Reflections of The English Medium

Reflections of The English Medium

Nigel Gaff

ISBN: 9798375372679

Dedications

In loving memory of my dear
Mother and Father.

Special Thanks

This book could never have been written without the hard work of my friends.

My big thanks and love to:
Gaye Smart,
Lynn Florkiewicz
and
Rodney Stenning.

You're all stars and I could not have done any of this without you and here's why:

When I left school I couldn't read or write, so this is somewhat of a miracle.
I never thought in a million years that I would ever write a book.
So, there you go.
You never know what's possible in your life until you try.

Acknowledgements

This book was written with the professional guidance and services of author Terri Stockley-Hetherington.

Forward

Before I go any further, I would like to take a moment to emphasise a few things here.

Firstly, what I have written in this book is the absolute truth as I know it. My experiences, however far removed they may sound at times, are what has actually happened to me. Not anyone else. Me.

Secondly, I am sharing with you what knowledge I have gained over my lifetime so far, in this life and many more before. I am a profound believer that we live many lives and are reincarnated many times until we have found what our soul desires.
I cannot say that I have visited Heaven, or that I know, for a fact, with proof, that there is life after our physical death here on this earthly plane. But, I can tell you now, in no uncertain terms, that I *believe*, deep down in my soul, that it is true. I know because I can communicate with those who have lived here before, but have passed back to the spirit realm.

My experiences are proof enough for me.

Introduction

My name is Nigel Gaff and I talk to dead people.

That always makes me smile, because there's no better way of stopping a conversation, especially if you don't want to talk to someone.
However, it can also be a bit of an ice breaker, I guess.

The fact is, if I can communicate with spirits, just as all mediums do, they're not dead.

So where is death?
Simple truth is, the is no death.
We do not die.
We simply evolve.

And how do I know this? I hope this book will help you understand what I have learned and now know. I want to share my secrets with you.

Those who are interested ask me questions about what I see or hear and the work I do.

During my demonstrations, I always try and make time for questions because people are inquisitive about it all; but, in this short period of time, it's impossible to cover everything.

So, this is why I've written this book and I hope you enjoy reading the result.

If you have any questions, you can contact me while I am still alive, otherwise you'll have to find a Medium!

Remember, we're all stuck with this thing called "life".

The chances are, if you're reading this,
you're still alive.
Make sure you make the best of it.

Life is for the living - the dead take care of their own.

Contents

Who Am I?

I Am The English Medium

Hi!

My name is Nigel Gaff and I am a The English Medium.

Essentially, this means (as I said in the forward of this book – but who reads that bit anyway?) that I talk to dead people, or the spirits of people who have now passed on.

I would call myself a conduit, a connection, a messenger. I have links to the spiritual realms.

Now, I find that people are either fascinated, terrified or immediately dislike what I do, but, to me, it's normal.

I'm not religious and I don't go door knocking. I don't force my beliefs on other people; I never would. It is people that come and find me.

I have been asked many, many questions over the years, about my work, how I came to learn of my gift and develop it and what happens when I connect with the spiritual realms.

This book was written with all of those questions in mind, with the hopes of answering most of them.

I have, over many years now, used my gift to help spirits of those no longer living on this earthly plane to connect with loved ones who are still here, to send messages of love and peace.

To be honest with you, I think some of the stories that you will read in this book may be hard to believe. They are even hard for me to believe, and I am the one who experienced them! I know they are real but of course, someone reading this book isn't necessarily going to see it, so you can only take my word for it.

I am not a liar and dishonesty is something I deplore.

Coming Into The World

I feel that, to understand the work I do, I must first introduce you to the person I am and how I learned of my gift. And to know me, means that we have to go way back many years, even to before I was born into this physical realm.

My father, Frederick Jnr, was born and raised in Chesterfield. He and his brother and two sisters had a very strict upbringing as my grandparents were very religious. In fact, my Father and his siblings had to go to church three times on a Sunday. In hindsight, I can understand now why he was so against the spirit work I do. Religion really isn't the medium's biggest fan and I am sure there are still people out there that would still burn us if they could.

As children, he and his siblings we not allowed to listen to the radio or play board and card games. I felt a little sad for him in a way, but I think he had a happy childhood. I don't remember much about my Father's parents, but I do recall my grandfather, Frederick Senior, to be a kind and lovely man, even if he was a strict man. I believe he was a boxer in his time and served in the army. My paternal Grandmother was the stricter of the two.

After his schooling, my father began an apprenticeship in printing, however, before he could finish, he joined the Royal Air Force. During his service, my Dad was posted to India during World War II, fighting the Japanese on the Burma campaign, stuck with a gun in his hand, out in the jungle trying to stop being shot or captured by the Japanese. These were terrible times for young men the world over. Where is the love of our own species? No wonder life is short; our souls need a break from the pain of this world.

Dad was a brave man, as were all the men that found themselves in conflict. War is a terrible thing. He never spoke much about his experiences during the war, but he did witness some dark happenings whilst in Burma. It was whilst he was serving in the RAF when he met my mother.

My mother, Alice, was born and raised in Manchester, along with her brother and three sisters. My Mum also had quite a firm upbringing, but I don't believe her family were as religious as my Father's. I remember my maternal Grandmother being quite stern.

My Mother joined the Royal Air Force and made her way up to a silver service waitress, serving pilots and other military personnel.

My parents met when they were both stationed at North Luffenham RAF Base, in Rutland. My mum was actually previously engaged to a flight officer before she met my dad.

My parents courted for a while before marrying. They settled down in Chesterfield. Once both of my parents had left the Royal Air Force, my Father continued his apprenticeship in printing and my Mother stayed at home and took care of the house, as was quite common in those days.

Then, along I came!

I was born into this world, from my true home and leaving all my friends and God's love, on the 15th of January 1962.

Feeling old now.

Mum's Gift

It was only after my parents had married that my Dad found out that my Mum was a medium. This scared him so much. I think it was partly because he didn't understand it, but also because of his strict religious upbringing. This meant he wouldn't want this in the house, so much so, that he forbade her from ever doing any readings, clairvoyance or mediumship of any kind.

This was really sad for Mum because mediums are born into the work of being mediums. You can't take the average guy or woman off the street and turn them into a medium. It's either in you or it isn't and it clearly *was* in my Mother, so it was sad that she never worked with it.

It wasn't until I was around thirteen that I found out my mother was a medium.

I remember her telling me that before she met my Dad, she met a medium that was stationed with her in the officers mess at a fighter air strip during World War II. She and some friends went to see a lady for a reading. When it was my Mum's turn, she told her she wasn't going to marry the man she was engaged to (he was a flight officer). The medium said she could see another man and then went on to describe my Dad exactly.

She then told my Mum that she had the gift and all it needed was bringing out. Well, Mum was terrified. She went back to her accommodation; it was late, and everybody was asleep and she lay in bed thinking of what had been said.

And then it happened.

A man appeared at the end of her bed. He was wearing a turban and had olive skin. She nearly passed out with fear and spent the night under the covers, too scared to come out. The next day she re-visited the medium and told her of the encounter.

"Don't worry," she said, "it was just your guide showing himself."

She never forgot that and told this story many times.

There were many instances she told me about when she would have friends round and she would see things or see spiritual auras around them. I remember her telling me once that she did a reading for one of her friends, this was before my Dad knew of my Mum's gift.

It was a tea leaf reading, as years ago, they used to read the tea leaves. She would make them a cup of tea, the person would drink the tea, with only the leaves remaining in the bottom of the cup. She would turn the cup over in the saucer, turn it round three times and then read the leaves.

It's kind of like today where we use tarot cards, but they used tea leaves. Mum read her friend's tea leaves and told her everything right down to the man she was going to marry. She described him to a tee, excuse the pun! But when Dad found out about it, he put an end to it. That's when he forbade Mum from doing it; it scared him so much.

As I grew older, my Mum used to tell me some stories of her experiences but she never worked with her gift because of how my Dad felt about it all.

I do miss her.

Looking back, it was a shame that my Father wouldn't open up a little and learn of my Mother's gift, as, when I was growing up, maybe my Mother would have been able to better explain what was happening to me. Maybe I wouldn't have been so scared myself. But I don't and won't ever hold it against my dad. He was a good man, husband and father. And now that I am of the age I am, I understand the concerns and worries he had for my Mother. It was not something that he could protect her from.

My Early Years

As a small child, I had all sorts of experiences. These were mainly at night when the lights went out. It seemed that when the lights went out, people used to start talking to me and, to be quite honest, it scared the hell out of me. I would lay awake, under the cover, completely stiff and unable to move through sheer fear. I hated it. I had to have the lights on everywhere because I was so terrified. Spirits came out because I was relaxed and became more open and susceptible. But I was so young, I didn't know what or who they were, and I guess this added to my fear.

I think my Mum must have known what was going on with me, but she kept it quiet and away from Dad because he wasn't interested. Don't get me wrong, I'm not knocking my Dad. As I said before, he was a loving man, a good man and very kind to me. But as I grew, these experiences got strong and it would have been nice to speak with someone who understood or had had the same or similar experiences, like my Mum.

I remember having some awful nightmares, almost every night, with people coming into my room and standing or sitting on my bed and, as a young child, I found this really terrifying.

I can't tell you how scared I was. I remember crying out in the middle of most nights. Mum used to come in and nurse me back down and tell me it was just a dream and not to worry.

But, even at such a young age, I knew it was more than just a dream. It affected me greatly in this life.

What I didn't understand at that time, was that spirits were only coming around me because they loved me. They wanted to be with me but, as a young boy, I was so scared. I can see now that it wasn't that they were trying to hurt or scare me, they were just trying to make me aware of them.

As children grow up and reach about five or six years old, perhaps a bit older, they lose the gifts of clairvoyance, mediumship and spirituality. It closes down. The energy points, the seven major chakras, close down because the soul feels itself in the physical body.

You feel your feet on the floor and you realise you have a life and the spiritual side of you closes and shuts down. I'd like to bet just about all of you have had some spiritual experience in your life, mostly as a young child. It's normal.

You've probably seen it in your own children. Often, they will have imaginary friends when they're young and, as parents, we put that down to them having a good imagination. The chances are, they're spending time with a relative or a child spirit that just wants to play.

My parents moved around quite a lot with Dad's work as a printer. We moved from Chesterfield, in Derbyshire, when I was two, maybe three years old, down to Newbury, in Berkshire, where I started school. I quite liked it there in Newbury and made friends with other kids in the street.

Mum, however, hated living in there. She suffered badly with depression, and she found it difficult to make friends. She just couldn't settle there; she put a lot of weight on and was very unhappy. I don't think my Father found this time very easy himself either.

After several years, Dad took a managerial job in Caerphilly, in South Wales. As I remember back, spirits and spiritual energy have followed me around, everywhere we have lived. Unlike Newbury, I hated Caerphilly because I found it difficult to make friends and got into lots of fights at school.

In those days, English people weren't as welcome as they are today. We had some hostility, from having our washing nicked off the line, milk taken from the doorstep, to Dad getting shot with an air rifle! Due to all the thefts, Dad bought an Alsatian for protection but this dog bit everyone in the family systematically and unfortunately, we had to rehome him somewhere else. Fortunately, times have changed and some of my good friends are from Wales.

When I was around eight or nine years of age, we abruptly left Wales and moved back to England, to Crawley in West Sussex, to be precise. At the time, I couldn't remember why we moved so suddenly, but years later, it would all come back to me. The reason we moved home so quickly, was because I had told my Father that I was being sexually abused by neighbour of ours. At the time, he had groomed me, made me feel special and gave me a beautiful wooden sailing boat that actually sailed on the water. He said it was a gift because I was his 'good, special boy', but it was just a way to lure me into his devious, sinful ways.

I had blocked it all out. My mind, not able to process the abuse, had blocked it out with a black cloak, shielding my soul from the pain. It was a natural, subconscious, protective instinct. It was many, many years later, through a 'Matrix Reimprinted' course that I gained access to these memories and began to properly process what had happened to me. But I'll come back to this later.

I started a new junior school in Crawley and we seemed to settle in okay, better than we had in Newbury or Wales.

Teenage Trials And Triumphs

Before long, I started secondary school and hit my teenage years. I didn't really have many friends at school, preferring my own company. I think now, looking back, I had trust issues from the abuse I had received, but I was too young to understand that, and I'd also blocked those memories from my conscious mind.

Being a teenager was tough most of the time, if I'm completely honest. Both my parents were quite strict, more so my Dad. If I was late home by even five minutes, he'd come looking for me! It was around this time that my Dad quit the printing industry and started up his own decorating company.

When I was a young teenager, I was taken to the doctor because I kept getting negative thoughts; scary pictures of people dying; of bad accidents; and it traumatised me. I got them all the time. These thoughts came and I didn't know what to do about them. I found it difficult to shut off. So, I ended up at the doctor's and he explained that this wasn't normal, and we needed to do something about it. I was quite pleased actually, as he made an appointment for me to see the in-house psychiatrist.

When I got to see the psychiatrist, there was nothing about him that I found helpful. He gave me no help at all and I felt he was more depressed than I was. I'd never seen a healthcare professional before; this was my first encounter. He simply wasn't what I expected and I thought he would understand me and offer me constructive advice. But he didn't seem able to – he seemed odd to me. I was a young teenager interested in girls and motorbikes and this was a middle-aged man that had no answers, only anti-depressants.

But I wasn't depressed. So, the medication did nothing for me and I was still getting these negative thoughts.

Only now, I was beginning to see things in the future.

I was seeing events before I even knew about them. For instance, I remember that my Dad received a phone call from my auntie Gladys to say that my uncle Les had died. Before that, I knew the phone would ring, I already knew my Uncle had died because I'd seen him, and I knew it was uncle Les that had passed on.

In the end I realised that I wasn't going mad. I had a realisation that these thoughts and images weren't mine. They were other people's and they had been passed on to me. It was the *essence,* or *energy* of the person that I was experiencing. What was happening to me was, that I was seeing spirits, or dead people if you like. This is when I began to talk to them as if they were here, and I found that they spoke right back to me. Now, when I say 'spoke' right back to me, what I mean is that I could see images in my mind that helped them to communicate with me.

At first, they terrified me! I was communicating with the dead! But now, I'm not scared. Not anymore. It's all about knowledge and fear; gain the knowledge and lose the fear. Unfortunately, it took me years to work that out! So, at the time, because I was scared still, I chose to block it all out. Selectively ignoring the visits from spirits and the unwanted images that popped into my mind occasionally. I wanted nothing more than to be a normal teenager. I didn't realise or understand at that age the gift I had been blessed with. For those years, it didn't feel so much of a gift as it did a curse. But blocking it out did help. For a few years too.

A Young Man

When I left school at the young age of sixteen, I left with not a single qualification. I could not read or write. I had found my years at school very difficult. But I did manage to make a couple of friends.

My Dad offered me a job working with him in his company as a decorator/handy man. I was grateful for this opportunity as I gained a lot of knowledge and experience from my time working with my Dad.

I was around seventeen when I passed my driving test. It meant that I was the first to drive out of my small group of friends. I didn't mind being a chauffeur and driving us all about town. It was good fun!

I remember my friend Kevin; he was going out with a young lady at the time and he wanted to double date. So, he set me up on a blind date with his girlfriend's cousin! I drove down to pick her up, drove all the way back to the pub for a double date and drove her back home afterward! Of course, I didn't drink! Well, the date went brilliantly! We hit it off straight away and within weeks we became inseparable, spending every minute we could with each other.

I never told my good friends or my girlfriend about my gift. At the time, I was still blocking it out as much as I could, getting on with my life as best I could.

About a year or so later, my parents announced that they were moving back up North. I didn't want to go. I felt that I had a life in Crawley. I had a wonderful girlfriend, a couple of good friends and I felt settled, happy even. After a few discussions, the decision was made that I would stay in the house and my parents would put the tenancy into my name, and they would continue with their plans to move. They packed up almost the entire contents of the house and left.

Suddenly, I felt very lost and lonely. I had no idea how to pay the bills, or who to pay them to. I had very little furniture and now I was also without a job. I found it very difficult to manage on my own at first. The house was awfully quiet, and it took some getting used to.

It was then that I started up my own business. A renovation and refurbishment business to be precise. I felt confident enough to do so, what with all the knowledge and skills that I had learned from working alongside my Dad.

My relationship with my girlfriend went from strength to strength, so much so that, at age twenty-one, I proposed and we got married in Worth Church in Crawley. We made the house our home and went on to buy it.

A Psychic (Af)Fair

Around three years after we married, my Wife and I sold the house and we moved into a house in Crawley. We stayed there for a few years making the most of the ever-rising house prices and eventually we made a tidy profit.

But I had restless feet and wanted more, so we sold up and bought a semi-detached house that needed a lot of work doing to it. It had been occupied by older people prior to us and they hadn't done much in regards to renovating the property, so it needed a new kitchen and bathroom.

We didn't have any children at that point and I remember how I loved the look of the house from the start. I sat outside just staring at it and thinking that this house was the one for me. I don't know why it was calling to me; I simply remember that it felt so right and I knew I would live there.

Though financially it was a massive stretch for us buying the house, I knew we would live there. I was in my mid-twenties and I was over the moon about buying this house. This was where my spirituality really took off; the house was so haunted it was like a Hollywood film; there were energy lines running all over the place!

This house was in a small village near Crawley, called Ifield. Ifield is one of the oldest parts of Crawley and appears in the Doomsday Book – you can imagine the wonderful history there.

I had made a study for myself upstairs in a small box room. It suited me. We had no kids as of yet and it gave me somewhere to work. You won't believe this, but I bought a book on how to build computers and I built my own. I bought a 19 inch monitor and, to my amazement, I turned it on and it worked!

It is in this house where spirits would make themselves felt so that I could begin my work as a medium, and so that I would understand this way of life.

The house was literally like Piccadilly Circus. There were spirits wandering in and out all day long and, of course, I didn't have the awareness to understand. I knew there was something going on in there but, for the life of me, couldn't work out what.

Up until this time, I had not told my wife of my gift. However, she was sensitive to the energies flowing through the house and it was then that seemed the opportune moment to tell her. It's strange but, she wasn't at all surprised. It wasn't something she wanted to really know more about, but she was aware she had a gift herself.

Not all people who are born mediums want to use or develop their gift, which is totally understandable. It is difficult at times, to feel the energies of another spirit. It can be emotionally and mentally draining.

Anyway, one weekend, there was a psychic fair on at a local theatre in Crawley. I'd never been to anything like it in my life before, but for some reason, I knew that I had to go. There were crystal stalls, tarot readers, healers, aura photography and so much more.

There was a chap who was sat at the back of the room who was doing personal readings with tarot cards. I looked at him. There was something so very different about this man compared to everybody else. It's hard to explain. He just seemed to generate some kind of energy. I didn't understand it, but I felt drawn to him.

So, I put my name down to have a reading by him. There was a long queue, so I went off, had a coffee and wandered around the show. I felt very at home there and I had a strange feeling, one that I had not experienced before; I suppose you could call it contentedness.

The medium I had booked to have a reading with, stood up and did a demonstration of mediumship to an audience and I was just amazed. He brought through people who had passed on; people who had died, which was hard to believe at first, but once he started giving evidence which was accurate beyond belief, I found it fascinating. He gave specific details, descriptions, names, symptoms, places etc; information about the deceased person's lives that he could not have possibly known. He also told some members of the audience what was going to happen in the future, that no one knew, but he felt this was going to be the case.

I guess I should have been shocked but I wasn't. It all felt strangely normal to me.

My time arrived and I had a reading with him, and he told me things that he just could not have possibly known. He told me about my life, my relationship, how I was going to have children, and it simply blew me away.

During the tarot reading, I became aware of a presence around me. But this wasn't like the usual energies I had felt before. This was a more loving and nurturing spiritual energy. It was a Native American man in full traditional dress. But, at that moment, I didn't have a clue who he was.

After that reading I became hooked. I went out and started buying books on spirituality and for the first time in my life, I felt that I had found a calling.

This gentleman, the medium that read my tarot cards and told me about my life, was Peter Richards. We became close friends and have stayed so ever since; in fact, we work together occasionally doing evenings of mediumship and I feel really honoured that he has chosen me as a fellow medium. He really is a very special man.

Peter introduced me to a lady who ran the psychic fairs and ran a shop in Crawley. She was running a development group, also known as a 'circle', to learn about tarot cards, meditation and generally introducing people to their psychic abilities. I sat with her and learned things for the best part of a year after that night.

However, it was that reading with Peter that opened the door.

The Foundations

Sitting In Circle

Now that I had met Peter and had a reading with him, my mind was open, and I was desperate to know more. I wanted to learn more about my gift and how to use it. I wanted to meet more spiritual people. I wanted to gain more knowledge.

I read as many books as I could and attended more psychic fairs. I met with more spiritualist believers, and I felt 'at home', like I 'belonged'.

As I was saying, I had become hooked. Okay, I was pretty much obsessed by this time.

I needed to learn more!

So, I began by attending a development circle, run by the lady I had met at my first psychic fair in Crawley.

A circle is just a small group of like-minded people who sit together with someone who sort of teaches or guides the group, normally a professional medium, who has spiritual knowledge, to help you open up, to link you in with your spiritual guides and to aid you in understanding your unique and individual spiritualistic experiences.

In these circles, I discovered tarot cards, learned of chakras and healing. I done some aura work, psychometry (this is where we are given an object, a piece of jewellery for example, and see if we have any energies come through) and sand readings. I thoroughly enjoyed it all and I soaked up all this new information.

Finally, I felt that I was no longer running away from the apparitions or trying to block out the unwanted images. I finally understood my calling. My gift wasn't so much my gift. It was a gift to others. I was a passage between the spiritual realms and this earthly, physical realm. I was a messenger, and I was passing on messages of love, peace and happiness.

It was around this time that I completed my Reiki Master Healing level 1. At the same psychic fair that I had met Peter, I had met a Reiki Master. He was a well presented, shaven headed man, a Buddhist. We had come to talking and it was with him that I ended up doing my training with! Can you believe that?

I've said it before and I will say it again, there are no coincidences in this life. We are meant to meet the people we do.

Anyway, I spent the good part of a year working with this lady from Crawley in her development circles, and I am thankful for the experiences and all that I learned in my early days of mediumship.

To learn Mediumship is a slow-burning candle. Knowledge and understanding are two different things. You can have all the knowledge in the world but, to understand it, you have to live it and experience it.

This is a gradual process.

A Valuable Lesson

Unfortunately, the lady who ran the development circle in Crawley that I had been attending, well, let's say, I don't think she had enough knowledge to be able to protect me or understand what she was really doing.

Consequently, I had a bad experience.

I developed very quickly at first and I remember, around a year or so into joining the circle, I was sitting with her when we were learning the tarot cards. With the greatest respect to her, she was quite good with them; but that particular night I remember how we were working above her shop and downstairs I could feel a presence. I could actually feel energy at the bottom of the stairs, which I sensed was looking up at us.

I made a big mistake and I got involved with it all. When I say got involved, I mean that I tried to communicate with it. It was a man. A tramp to be precise. I was running before I could walk and without the knowledge to protect myself; a common mistake.

Well, this gentleman followed me home and became a bit of a nuisance for a while. Now, with hindsight, this was all meant to be.

It was designed to slow me down.

I was trying to run before I could walk, as the saying goes. I wanted to learn so much, that I was trying to take too much in at once, and although I was gaining knowledge, I wasn't necessarily gaining the experience I needed to fully grasp and understand the knowledge I was taking in.

The effect it had on me was to slow me down to a snail's pace so that my learning almost halted. This was meant to be, as one of my old teachers said 'you need to take the goods train, not the express. You need to see so much, and you need to see it all several times again as well, to understand it all and learn'.

There is a great deal that mediums need to learn to work as mediums; it is a very involved job and there is a lot of learning to do; actually, we are always learning; every minute of every day, we are taking in new information. Anyway, it all got sorted in the end, thankfully. The lady whose circle it was, well, I told her about the bad energy that had somehow latched itself to me that night. I know she felt bad and somewhat responsible for what had happened, so she paid me a visit and helped me get rid of the unwanted energy.

But, it slowed me down, just as it was meant to.

It was just a real shock to me to start with.

Healing Circle

After my bad experience with the tramp energy, I never returned to that development circle. It just didn't feel right. But as luck, or fate, would have it, my good friend Peter started up his own development circle, which I attended.

It was during a meditation session in one of these development circles that I properly met my Native American guide, the one who had appeared to me at my reading with Peter. I didn't know who he was then, but now he was there, saying hello and letting me know he was one of my many guides. He told me his name was Morning Cloud.

A few months later, I visited another psychic fair and there was a psychic artist there. A psychic artist is someone with strong clairvoyant ability (and artistic drawing ability!), able to transfer the spirit image onto paper.

Amazing!

Not only could she see him, but she drew him. She drew the exact image of the man I had seen before, during my tarot reading with Peter and during my meditation. Literally spot on! Her name was Doris Strode and she drew my Native American guide, Morning Cloud, very accurately and she was very good. I think they were all making me aware of who they were and, as a race of people, I find them really interesting.

"In this world, mediums stand alone. They do so because they have to." I will never forget that statement that an old friend of mine, also a medium, said many years ago.

Here in life, mediums often have some of the hardest lessons to learn. That is sad to say but nevertheless it's true. And the reason is that it is to teach the medium to help them understand other peoples' lives. It gives the medium more empathy to be able to better help them.

For example…

You don't know the flame is hot until you put your hand in it and you can feel it. You can be told a hundred times that it will hurt but you must experience it to truly understand. Knowledge and understanding are two different things.

That's why it takes many years to become a medium, because there is so much that you have to learn; you have to take the goods train and not the express. If you want to learn quickly, you take the express; but you're going to have to go all the way back to the beginning, again, and relearn everything.

You see, when you are on the goods train, it is going slowly and you can look out of the window and take in all the information that is there for you to absorb and see. When you're on the express train, it just rattles past so fast that you only get glimpses of it all, so you must go back to the beginning and relearn it all over again.

Every time I run a circle and I teach, whether it's my spiritual work, mediumship and clairvoyance or whether it's working with somebody's mind, I learn and am still learning.

I will forever be learning.

I pick up more information and gain more and more input from the spiritual realms as well. The more and more I do it, the more versed I get in it and gain more understanding; because knowing something and understanding something are two completely different things.

That is why it takes a long time to become a medium, many years of experiencing and understanding.

Even though you may have gone through many years of growth, understanding and learning, when you start working with it, you find you have to start learning all over again.

About a year or so later, I had stopped going to Peter's development group by this time as I felt I was able and confident enough to learn, grow and progress further on my own.

I felt that I had evolved enough spiritually to lead my own healing group.

There were about twelve or thirteen of us. Every Friday night we would sit together and give and receive healing and meditate on healing and it was truly wonderful.

There is never any charge for someone to attend a healing group.

This was when I met another of my guides, Dr Feligrew (I will talk more about my guides a little later). He is my healing guide.

It was during my time running the healing circle that I went back to complete my levels 2 and 3 in Reiki Healing and became a Reiki Master.

I gained a lot of wisdom in those first few years of embracing my gift and spirituality. The next few chapters are what I call 'The Foundations', and they are, indeed, the building blocks of my beliefs.

Energy

I want to talk about energy. Energy is the fundamental building block of all, you see.

Everything is energy.

You're energy, I'm energy, everything that we see has its own energy.

Our energy is unique only to us.

The happier we are, the more vibrant our energy and we attract more of the same.

Your energy is, collectively, your entire soul, your complete subconscious.

It is your spirit.

The GOD Energy And Reincarnation

"Why would you want to come back here to the physical plane if it's so wonderful there in the spiritual realms?"

Well, there lies the question, my friend.

The reason is because of where you are from.

As beautiful as it is, if you look up, you'll find that there are more levels and those levels are filled with even more beautiful things.

You look and can stretch your neck all the way up and you can see the greatest, whitest light. This is the God energy, the power sitting as far up as it goes and you know that you want to get there; you want to get to where all the action is happening. You want to get to where God is doing creative work, so you can be part of that but you also realise that, to get there, you need to learn more; your soul needs to expand, develop and grow. The quickest, sharpest way for your soul to expand and grow is to have a life.

There is no doubt about that.

So that's why you have this life and that's why you'll have more, as well, as you start to expand, and your spirit starts to grow. You will realise, "hey, I want to go where God is because that's where all the action is!"

Wouldn't it be wonderful to join with the Creator and start building new worlds, creating new species and building new galaxies? How fantastic would that be? And you can be part of that; but to be part of it you're going to have to expand your soul. To do that, a life is the quickest, shortest and the most effective way of all and will give you the best optimum results when you get home, back to the spiritual realms.

There are other ways to grow. Some spirits never come out of spirit realms. They stay there forever and a day, they still grow, and they reach different levels but it takes so much longer, so much more patience, so much more commitment. Whereas, a life is the quickest way of doing it, so you should be celebrating your life and thinking, well, you know what, you're doing better for yourself spiritually.

Of course, you can also walk with someone. Sometimes spirits will come to an earth plane, and they will walk with an individual and they will follow the footsteps basically behind you all your life. They will tread your footsteps exactly as you have trodden and they will try and learn everything you're learning.

They do that to try and understand and grow as well. But, ultimately, the way to grow the quickest is here.

This is where the action is.

This is where the main event, the real deal is. That's why you're here, and that's why you've had a lot of lives and that's why you'll have many more. It's a difficult one to comprehend or even believe, but it's not until you get home that you see that to be the truth for yourself.

You see, when you're born, your mind is wiped of all your experiences of where you're from. If it didn't wipe clean, it would be a pointless exercise in being here. It would be a pointless journey to live a life with all the knowledge of where you're from. A life is the quickest way for your soul to grow. It ascends much quicker and I would say just about 99.9 percent of the world's population has a hard life; we all do. I've had so many difficulties and traumas and I'm sure everybody reading this book has had their problems too.

You ask yourself, why?

Why, if God was real, would he let me go through this? But it is because God is real and because he does love you, this is the reason you are going through it all. This helps your soul grow so that you can ascend to reach the God energy when you go home.

That's why life is short; it is short, it's a painful trip but, it's over and done with quickly. You go home and you're able to then look at your life in the greatest of detail and other lives you've had as well. Once you've looked at all of those lives, then, after a period of time (though time doesn't exist in the spiritual realms, time is an illusion, it's manmade), nine out of ten, you will make a decision to come back and have another go, to maybe relearn what you didn't learn in this life, the life you are currently living.

Or maybe you're here to learn something completely different; for instance, to learn what it is like to be disabled, to be rich or poor, to experience all you can in a life. You can experience pleasure and pain, sadness and sorrow, happiness and excitement.

This is what life is.

It's for your soul's growth. It is not for your conscious being. Your conscious being is purely being led down the garden path to think that this is all there is.

It isn't. This is just one dimension and it's not your true dimension, it operates outside of the parameters of true reality.

The only real and true dimension is where you are from and where you go back to. There are many accounts, over many years, of people who have died, seen a glimpse of the spiritual realms and came back, because it wasn't their time. But they've seen things that they just can't explain, such as a pure, brilliant white light, their loved ones who have passed, and the most wonderful, beautiful things, because there is nothing there in the world of spirit that there is here.

It is a structure of spirit; it is a dimension that is unknown to us because it has to be. If you truly knew how beautiful and how wondrous it is there, you wouldn't want to stay here any longer, would you? You wouldn't want to put up with pain and sorrow and unhappiness. You'd want to go back there because there is nothing more than love. There is no such thing as pain and sadness, and there is no suffering.

There are dimensions that you exist in, within the spiritual realm, that are bigger than the universe and galaxies that you can explore. It is truly wondrous and what's even more amazing is that the life you're having now is driving you towards a greater goal in spirit. This life is feeding your soul and although you don't realise it, you are becoming more than you could ever imagine.

Every life that you live will take you closer to the God energy.

That is the whole idea.

When you are standing in the spiritual realms and you look up, the white light is so intense. That's where the God energy lies, and that's where you want to get to. With Him, with Her, with the Creator, because that's truly Heaven up there.

The closeness of love that you experience when you're home, in spirit, can never be anything like the love you feel here in this life.

The closest I can come to that is the love and the feeling of oneness which a mother feels for her child. That's getting close to it because it is such an all-encompassing, overwhelming feeling that spirit gives you.

They love you. They truly do and they know how hard it is here for you. They understand and they do appreciate that; they really do.

So, you go back to spirit, and you rest and you understand and you grow and you'll probably come back here or another planet to have another life and experience and learn even more.

Happy days.

Therefore, you truly are immortal. You have more chance of winning the lottery every week for the rest of this life than you do of dying - it just won't happen.

Your physical body will perish but what you truly are will never finish.

And I hear you ask, how do I know these things? Well, I just know them. I know them very accurately because they're memories I have in my subconscious, which, for some reason, I have access to, just as all mediums do. We all have access to different knowledge in our subconscious minds which relates to our spirituality and to our spiritual existence and the spiritual realms.

What Is Death?

What is death?

What happens when you're dead?

What happens when your life is finished, when the spirit can no longer stay within the body, the body is broken beyond repair and things just stop working?

What happens to the soul then?

Now that I have explained what we are, energy, I hope you have more of an understanding of what happens when we die, or at least, when the physical body that we inhabit here in this physical realm, ceases to work and no longer holds our energy, our soul.

Well, as our physical body dies, or energy, our soul or spirit, leaves the body, but as it does, it still retains the same image, or identity as the body it has just left. It still has arms, legs, and a head; all very much complete in terms of the form from which it has recently left. But it transcends back into the spirit realms and you turn back to what you truly are, which is light. That is what your spirit is. You're seen and known by your light, by your colour and that's how spirit recognises each other.

When you are born into this physical plane, when you leave the spiritual realms to come here or to a world like this, spirit mourns your passing from their realms. Although they know that you're leaving, they also know they're going to see you again.

Then, of course, when we have a child born here in the physical plane, we celebrate the birth. It's wonderful, a new born baby has come in to this world. But spirit are mourning the passing from their realms into this physical world of one of their own.

Of course, it works the other way round too.

Whenever we pass from here, when our time has come, then our loved ones who we leave behind mourn our passing; they mourn us going back to the spiritual realm and, leaving them; they miss us terribly. And of course the opposite applies going back to spirit because there's a huge party, a massive celebration welcoming you back, welcoming you back home to where you truly, truly belong, and that's the most wonderful thing.

So although people say 'you win or you lose', truly you never ever lose. When you're alive you're winning, and when you're dead you're winning because you are going home, back to something that is so amazingly beautiful, wonderfully beautiful, you can't believe it. You won't understand any of it until your time has come.

None of us will.

As much as I've described and explained things, you have to have your own experiences.

In all the years I've done this work, I've never had any spirit come back and tell me they don't like it where they are. I've never had one of them complaining. Don't get me wrong, I've heard them moaning about their lives and I've heard them swearing as they would have done here, but not about where they are *now*.

They've been moaning about their existences here, moaning about the people in this world who aren't quite playing ball, but I've never heard them ever complaining about the spirit realms and where they're from.

How could you complain about something that's so wonderful?

Spiritualism Versus Religion

I said previously that I don't feel that religion and spiritualism get along.

I have many thoughts on this.

Now, I believe in God, or God energy. God, to me, stands for Grand Order of Design. I don't see God as a person, more the highest level of energy and creativeness.

The all-knowing Creator.

Religion, in my eyes, is man-made; constructive guidelines, as it were, with the aims of controlling humankind to some degree. We are only told of God, or Allah, or whichever deity it is that one cares to preach to, but no-one alive today can profess to meeting them.

Religious books have been written as rules, as a measure of control. But they are just books. There are millions of books in the world, how on earth can I take just one to be the 'ultimate truth'?

In my current life, I have seen more war, bloodshed and death in the name of religion than through any disease. It breaks my heart to see people maimed, tortured or killed in the name of religion.

Yet, I have never seen anyone die because of spiritualism.

You do not have to go to a church, a mosque or any other building, or read a specific book to be a spiritualist. You do not have to restrict your diet or stop doing things you enjoy in the name of spiritualism.

It does not matter where you were born, how old you are, the colour of your skin or what political party you support, spiritualism is open and available to everyone and anyone.

In my opinion, being a spiritualist means spreading love, joy and happiness; being understanding and offering kindness to those less fortunate.

What is interesting, is that I have friends and colleagues who are mediums who don't work with it. Although it's there and has been from childhood, they've ignored it and just let it pass by. They won't work with it and often it's a religious reason because they were brought up when they were young into a religious family. This sets up a conflict within them which says: 'You know, talking to the spirit world or to spirit is wrong', when in reality of course, it isn't wrong. Yet they feel they shouldn't work with it because it's not in their religion to talk to spirit.

There have been vicars and priests over the years who have had mediumistic ability, and who could work with spirit. You can imagine the massive emotional disharmony within them if they have this yearning to do mediumship and spiritual work but can't because their religion says it's wrong.

So, this starts the questioning of religion.

I was doing a demonstration one time, in a Spiritualist Church and a lady's grandfather came though. This man had been shot in the head on the Somme battlefield in World War I.

As the soldier stood within me, I watched his body fall. I could feel myself going too. I remember thinking: 'Oh here we go, but where do I go now?' I could see him looking around and seeing all these other dead soldiers with their bodies laying sprawled on the battlefield; however, they were looking at each other and trying to work out what had happened. They really didn't realize they were dead. A quick passing, finding themselves detached from their bodies, must have come as a big shock and also realizing they weren't dead must be a bit mind blowing especially if they were brought up with religion and had no understanding of spiritualism.

Religion, I believe, has lost its place in this world.

It has lost its place because it doesn't answer the really fundamental questions about *why* we're here. It just comes up with a romantic notion but that isn't true reality.

You are a different species to how you present yourself now. You are in fact, if you consider it, almost an alien. You are something more beautiful than you could ever conceive or imagine. You have more love in you than you could ever understand because you have the God energy in you and the God energy is pure love.

And that's what you bring here with you.

You are only here to experience fear so that you can learn and grow.

What Is Your Soul?

The subconscious mind is your spirit; it's your soul; it's your living essence; your unique energy; it's you. It is what you are; it makes you the individual you are now. Without your subconscious mind which is, in fact, your soul, you cease to exist.

I did a study which I found quite interesting to do with autism.

Now I find autism fascinating because these people find it difficult to exist in this reality. And yet usually, autistic children and grown-ups have an ability beyond ours to be able to do amazing things naturally and so fast and accurately.

I've looked at it and I couldn't quite work out why they are able to do this, but I've come to my own conclusion and that is that the soul, the subconscious mind, is closer to their consciousness here than ours.

You could drop a load of knitting needles out of your hand and before they hit the floor, the autistic person can know how many there are as they fall to the floor, just like Dustin Hoffman from the film Rain Man. It's because the subconscious mind works at light speed.

This is your soul, it's your energy and it's able to process information at light speed. Autistic people have a conscious mind that is not as effective as ours, it doesn't work like ours. Yet the subconscious, or the soul, in autistic people is closer to the conscious. This enables them to do the genius things they can do because that's where the genius lies; it's your subconscious/soul. That's how that works and it's absolutely fascinating – well, I think it is and hope you do too.

There is an American gentleman, Kim Peek, who was in a documentary programme. He is able to recount every single book he's ever read. He can tell you exactly what's on any given page. Give him the page number in the book, and he can tell you exactly what the fourth line down and what the third word along is. He's got that map in his subconscious and finds it normal to access that information.

What Kim can do is amazing. After reading over 12,000 books, he can recall everything about them. He's known as "Kimputer," and can read two pages at once. His left eye reads the left page, and his right eye reads the right page. It takes him two or three seconds to read two pages - and it is committed to his memory. He can recall facts and trivia from several areas including history, geography and sports. Give him a date and he'll tell you what day of the week it was. He can also remember every piece of music that he's ever listened to.

We all have that. We just can't access it in the same way that these special autistic people can. They are able to access this information perfectly but they're not all the same. Their ability to do things is different, depending on who they are and how severe their autism.

I think it's an interesting theory of mine. I don't think this is proven at all, it's not in print. Well, I don't think so anyway, it's just something that I have a great belief in.

Your soul, your subconscious mind, is the genius part of you. It's that which leaves your body when you die.

It's the true genius.

Nurturing The Soul

Your soul, your subconscious, is about five years old. It is just a child. Even though you could be an adult reading this, but your subconscious mind is nothing but a child.

If you want to get the best out of your life, if you want to get the most out of you, what's the best way to communicate to your subconscious mind?

The best way is to talk to it as you would to a child. Show it love and compassion because the greatest thing you can do in this life with your soul, your subconscious, is to love yourself.

Love your soul and love who you truly are and then the magic can really start to take place here.

That is the thing with the human being, the one thing that is missing greatly here is love. This is not love of each other, but it is love of ourselves because, when we can truly love ourselves, right down to our toenails and to our hair follicles, then it's easy to love everyone else. Then the world will be a different place. But I feel, I truly feel, that is never going to be the case.

When you're born here, you bring the love of spirit with you. You bring it here and you come to experience it here. Everything negative in your life, all your bad thoughts, everything that's bad about the world is based upon fear. Everything good, everything that's positive comes from the good, from the God energy.

Ever since Mankind stepped on this planet there has been a personal internal battle between love and fear. Everything that is negative and destructive arrives from fear, everything that is beautiful and wondrous comes from love.

Unfortunately, the human being spends too much time focusing and anchoring the fear and that manifests itself in peoples' lives in different ways; through jealousy, anger and all the bad stuff. That is all fear, all self-doubt.

So, what needs to happen is to take all that away and get rid of that fear and self-doubt, and then inject self-love, self-belief, self-praise and your whole life can really change around.

You are, regardless of anything else, the most important person in your life, or you should be. If you're not and somebody else is, then you're only going to get what you're given.

You need to *be* the love for yourself because when you love yourself unconditionally, at the deepest level possible, it is then very easy for you to love others and for others to love you.

Happiness

"What are you truly looking for here? What do you truly want in this world?"

I sometimes find myself asking my students these questions. Of course, I get lots of answers back.

"I want love and a good relationship with my partner."

"I want a nice car."

"I want a nice house and I want enough money to pay the bills."

"I want to win the lottery."

These are just some of the many replies that I have had to those questions.

The truth is, that what you're really looking for in the depths of your soul, is happiness. That is what drives us to go and look for relationships and makes you go out and buy cars, stay in nice hotels, buy big houses and everything we do. We do it all to fulfil one need. And that need is happiness.

We are looking constantly to be happy and to feel loved. We think we can find happiness and this love outside of ourselves. We believe we can find this through a wonderful wife, a handsome husband, a successful business or wonderful health. We think we can find it in everything outside of us, when the truth is, that what you are searching for is already in you. You're just not looking in the right place.

You have been searching and probably always will be, looking for that fulfilment, looking for that love; always looking for that extra something to bring you that feeling of happiness.

My advice is stop looking and go inwards.

Internal reflection is the key to the lock.

When you finally realise that what you are searching for in your life already runs through you in abundance, and always has, then you can be truly free.

I get my students to spend some time looking within and to start building love for themselves.

When you build love for yourself to the point where you're the most important person in your life, and where you love yourself unconditionally, then you won't need the houses or cars, the money or relationships. You'll be quite happy just being on your own for the rest of your life, if that's what you want. You'll be happy because you would have finally found yourself.

I have to admit that I'm not there yet.

Love is already within you and it's always been there. You brought it with you from the spiritual realms, you just forgot you had it.

You, me, all of us, are of the God energy and as such we are all filled with its love.

I will give you a scenario; imagine I just picked you up and deposited you on a beautiful Caribbean beach and placed around you the greatest riches of man. I gave you the most fantastic body ever seen and the most beautiful face; I made you the most intelligent human being in the world. You have everything you ever desired and you are happier than you could ever imagine.

Then, one day, I come back and I pick you up and I drag you back to reality, back here, where you are now, and you had to go to work to earning a living and living your life.

You may be overweight, drink and smoke too much; perhaps you're in a bad relationship, in debt, and so on and so forth and life's story goes on and on.

What would you strive to do?

Well, you would try your very best, wouldn't you? Try your best to get back to that beautiful place and to get back to those wonderful feelings, where you were so loved and where you felt so good and so happy. Unconsciously, you're looking for everything you've left behind you, because that's where you've come from. You have come from the Caribbean beach; you've come from that love where you can do or have anything. You've arrived from that wonderful place and come here. Now what you're looking for from the depths of your soul is to replicate that in some way or another.

You can't replicate that because that's there and only a memory.

The best you can do, is to bring forth the love for yourself here, in this life. When you truly can drop to your knees with this feeling of the greatest love and appreciation for yourself, then you can truly be happy. Be happy with yourself and who you are, regardless of where you live, how much you earn, what your health is or what relationship you're in. Really, your happiness has no bearing on who you're with or what you have.

When you're in the most perfect place within you, then the world outside moulds itself to your vibrational energy. So, this physical material world starts to change around you, simply because you have found your true power; your God energy.

Once you have so much love going on inside and once you feel so fantastically happy with having found this loving, then the people around you start to change. They begin to see a change in you, the energy feeds into them and they feed from that energy and start to become happier in themselves. You can then bring more money to you and better, more fulfilling relationships. You become healthier, your skin clears and any ailments you have improve.

Once you can love yourself at that level, and I'm talking about a profound love which you may never have experienced for yourself yet, then you'll just find it is so wonderful and magnificent. As you reach that level your whole life becomes a beautiful place to be.

But, my friend, I tell you this; it's a difficult one to achieve, and you know what, it requires work; consistent work on a daily basis, that puts you first in your mind. It doesn't make you selfish; it doesn't make you greedy or jealous; it doesn't make you anything negative because you can't truly give to someone else lovingly in an unselfish way, until you have that love and unselfishness for yourself.

The Human Mind

I was diagnosed with Multiple Sclerosis (MS) in 2003 (I will come back to this a bit later in the book). For those who don't know, this is a neurological disease which affects the nervous system running down the spinal cord. This, in turn, relates to my movement and energy levels.

Due to my mediumship, I have always had a great interest in the human mind and how it works. Why we do what we do and why some people were seemingly more successful than others; richer than others and why some people could have better relationships with others. I couldn't work it out.

So, I had a bit of a quest. I read a lot, studied all sorts of different people and eventually ended up in front of Paul McKenna and Richard Bandler.

Now Paul McKenna is quite a famous hypnotist in the UK. I trained with him, and a man called Richard Bandler who, along with another gentleman called John Grinder, invented Neuro Linguistic Programming (NLP) back in the seventies. NLP is the study of human behaviour relating to the five senses.

With the help of that and many other techniques, I have learned how to re-programme the mind, and how we process information.

Now here is the "what the hell are you on about Nigel?" bit.

You see, you have two intelligences.

You have a conscious mind which is reading this book. That data is going in through your eyes and down into your hyper intelligence which is your subconscious mind – this is, in fact, your soul. Your subconscious mind then forms programmes. It picks up all the information that you experience consciously in this world.

You have five senses; what you hear, what you see, what you smell, what you taste and what you feel. From the moment you were born and opened your eyes, you began to learn and experience through these senses; all the information started to go through your conscious mind to the subconscious mind. This is just writing all the information onto your hard drive, and this continues to be written all the time you are alive. Your hard drive is your soul. And this is the reason you have a life. All the information you have here, all you have experienced is written on that soul, onto your subconscious mind which is your hard drive. Everything has to be captured here so nothing is wasted for your soul, it is encapsulated in the finest of detail, high definition.

When you pass away and you leave your physical body it is your hard drive, your subconscious, your soul, your unique energy, which is the thing that leaves and goes back to the spirit realm.

When you're home, you can look at the life you have had in the greatest detail. You can see exactly what you have learnt while you were here; exactly what you've experienced and what you've avoided. One day, you might make the decision to come back and have another go, another life, although that is a completely different subject.

It's quite fascinating because, through studying, they've found that the human being sees in pictures, remembers in pictures and constructs pictures through imagination. Throughout this book, as I describe things, your subconscious, the genius of your mind, starts to form pictures from what I've said. The subconscious is making pictures all the time. You'd never find your way home if you didn't have a picture of it in your subconscious.

If I asked you: "What colour is your car and what colour is your front door?", your eyes would go off to the left or right. Try it with someone. Ask them a question and watch their eyes. Eventually, they will have to look to find the stored pictures. What is happening is you're searching for the information. This happens almost instantaneously as your conscious mind searches the stored memories within the subconscious, your soul or hyper intelligence, until it finds the corresponding picture to the question. That's how you know what colour your front door is and the colour of your car.

We all run programmes of how to walk, how to drink, how to eat, how to drive a car, how to swim, how to ride a bike, etc. They're all programmes that you've learned that have formed and stored in the subconscious mind.

So, when you get on a bike, for instance, that programme ignites. The information runs up through the neural cortex and into the conscious mind where you naturally know what to do; but it's a programme and it had to be learnt; it had to be formed and it had to be installed.

You see, the thing is, your subconscious mind is genius; it's your soul, a completely separate intelligence.

When you go to bed tonight and you're closing your eyes, have you ever considered how your body is going to keep going and how you're going to wake up in the morning? Well, you know, none of us even consider it, we don't because we don't need to, because the intelligence of our subconscious, our soul, is running the show.

You just couldn't run everything with your conscious mind. If I gave you ten things to do consciously, to keep you alive, you'd be dead in thirty seconds because consciously you can't process the information. We simply aren't that clever.

We can only process up to seven to ten pieces of information consciously per second, and most of that information is lost because we can't concentrate on multiple things. I know your wife says she can - she's fibbing.

The subconscious mind processes millions of calculations and imaginations every second. It's genius; a hyper intelligence. I always think to myself, if it can do that to keep you alive, which it does, it fights disease, it makes your hair grow, fills your mouth with saliva, it reasons beyond your conscious comprehension; well, if it can do all that, what else can it do for us? This is indeed the real magic of us all.

Well, it can do pretty much anything.

If you're struggling with finances in your life, the chances are, you've got bad financial programmes running in your subconscious mind. They are the programmes where your dad said: "Well, when you leave school, if you work hard, you might be able to have your own car and get a nice house, but you'll have to work hard." So that's one programme where you think: "Oh well, I can't get anything in my life unless I work hard," which is a fallacy - you don't have to.

The other programme is that money's a bad thing; it's dirty; money's not good; rich people aren't nice people; rich people aren't happy. This is, of course, just one area of your life. And these are all programmes which were formed in your subconscious when you were young from what you experience.

For example, people that have flying phobias have either had a bad experience themselves or witnessed a traumatic event that creates a phobic response to flying. It then creates the programme in the subconscious mind so, when they think about flying, this fear comes along and restricts them, often ruining their lives.

But it doesn't have to be that way. You can reprogramme the subconscious mind. You can manipulate and change the programmes which exist within the subconscious. People ask me, "well, what does all this have to do with spirituality and the spiritual realm? `

Knowledge

If you can imagine, your fist is full of sand and all the knowledge in the world that you have is that fistful of sand. Then as you look around you, you realise that you are standing in the middle of the Sahara Desert. All that sand is knowledge and all you've got is a fistful; but look around at how much knowledge there is available to you, so much if only you'd open your eyes.

There is so much more that a human being can learn, so much more we can do, but we choose not to. We choose to stay quiet and not discover that to be explored.

I feel that slowly but surely, this species is changing, spiritualism is becoming far more of a life change, a lifestyle for so many people.

People are more interested with the advent of television, the different mediums, and the different spiritual shows that are on.

It is becoming more and more popular, and people are more interested in it. I don't feel though that the human race will turn to spirituality completely; there is too much fear here for that.

I think this world will burn out like many others have burned out way before we ever get to that stage. The human being is never going to progress beyond much of where we are now, in terms of our belief and our understanding. The reason is that it's not designed that way. As I said, there is too much fear here for our species to grow beyond much of where we are now, and I hate to say it but I feel religion has a lot to answer for.

This place is meant to be hard; it's meant to be difficult.

If you think back to what I said earlier, it's the way we best learn. The human being, and the soul, learns best when it's going through the hardest of times. The good thing for the soul is that it is untouched in the body. As it can't be touched, it can't be hurt, and this is the way it grows and learns constantly from life experiences.

The Law Of Attraction

The human being is so powerful; we are far more powerful than we have any right to know. Whatever you're thinking, whatever you feel emotionally, is what you are attracting to you and what you're putting out into the world.

So, if you suffer with a lot of fear and you are a fearful person, then you'll attract fear to you, just like a magnet. But if you're a very happy person, then you'll attract more happiness and happy people to you. If you're someone who suffers from depression, then you'll just end up having friends that become depressed or are depressive.

You know the old saying? 'Birds of a feather flock together'. Well, that's very true. Alcoholic friends are all alcoholics, drug addict friends are all drug addicts; that's why you must be very careful with your thoughts, constantly monitoring them; because what you put out into the universe is exactly what you will attract back. Everything that happens to you comes to you as a result of what you are putting out through your thoughts. And that's a fact and that's how it works. It's called 'The Law of Attraction'.

We are constantly manifesting in this dimension, and everything that has ever been invented has come out of somebody's imagination first. That's the process. We picture it, we see it and then we manufacture it. We manifest it in this third dimension.

The human mind is so enormously powerful that you are constantly reinventing yourself; you're constantly building your dimension around you with your thought processes. I'm not here to talk about all that too much as there are many books, and all sorts of courses that are available for people to study; but all I know is that it's a reality that happens and it's true that people manifest and draw towards them the way they feel and think.

And that's the truth.

In my work, I also like to give practical advice to people. You can read many books about many mediums, the lives they've had and the messages they have passed on, and some of them are truly fascinating. There's no doubt about it, there have been some fantastic books written and there are some fantastic mediums out there, but I also like to give people an understanding because, you know, the more of an understanding you have of your life and the more control you can have, the better it is.

The truth of the matter is, what we think about, we manifest. We are reality architects, and we create the reality around us. Everything is an internal process.

We think, therefore we become.

It's a fact.

We create our own reality whether we have a successful, wealthy, healthy reality, or if we have created the opposite, or a mixture of both. We are constantly in the creative process. You are either creating consciously or subconsciously.

We're always creating, always making and building things, and everything that's ever been invented had to be imagined in somebody's head first.

As I said, we're all in the creative process but we're all blissfully unaware of the truth that surrounds us all the time. And because you are part of God, you are part of the Creator. And, because you're part of the Creator, you have the ability to create and we all do it.

We all create really wonderful things and we create really horrible things depending on the programmes we have running in our mind, depending on your upbringing and your experiences. Rich people generally come from rich backgrounds. They've grown up in rich families and, because of this, they don't know any different; therefore, it's easier for them to become wealthy because it's inbuilt, it's a learned programme. And that's just like any other programme you've got; walking, talking; all these programmes you learn as a baby.

We are born with this basic programme which is highly sophisticated. It's the programme to keep the body alive and your subconscious mind, your soul, does this on a day to day basis without any conscious thought from you at all. When do you ever think about how your lungs or your heart are working? When do you ever think about your hair growing, about how you open your mouth or have tears in your eyes? None of us ever consider this.

Why should we when it happens automatically?

Well, it doesn't happen by magic and if you consciously had to try and do it, you would probably be dead in less than thirty seconds because you wouldn't be able to do it. You couldn't keep your body going consciously.

You can only process seven to ten bits of information in a second and beyond that everything is lost. But the subconscious mind (or your soul, your energy) processes billions and billions of pieces of information every second. Your soul is genius and it is part of the Creator and that's why it is so genius.

But everything else in your life you learn. You learn to be poor; you learn to be rich; you learn to be happy, and you learn to be depressed. You learn all different types and manner of things which you then use and process to be used as programmes in your life.

The good thing is that these programmes you're running don't have to be permanent. You don't have to put up with them. You can change and manipulate them, and you can make them different from what they were. You can alter them in many ways and it's a fact. It's true and it works astonishingly well. I have personally experienced this.

I've trained as an NLP master practitioner, a hypnotic practitioner and work with people with anxiety and depression and all sorts or issues in their lives. I realise that everything that goes on in someone's life has come from within them because they've manifested it to help them learn and grow here.

Your spirit wants to learn and grow.

If something bad happened to you in your life, then it's bad enough, but people spend the rest of their life reliving that main trauma repeatedly, always in pain.

Well, you don't have to.

You don't have to keep running that programme over and over again. You can adjust and manipulate it so that it doesn't play in the same way.

The thing is that your subconscious mind has a limitless ability to be able to store data. Millions and millions of bits of data and it can do this throughout your entire life quite successfully until the conscious mind starts to fail and we have diseases such as Alzheimer's or dementia. Then the mind starts to degrade. You begin to lose the conscious connection with the subconscious mind, and you don't see things in the way you did before. Therefore, the subconscious is then failing to receive the information through in the right way.

Now that's a sad fact but you need both parts of the computer. You need the conscious mind which is the ram (random access memory) in the computer and you need the subconscious mind which is the hard drive. The housing of the computer is the human body. It's strange how we have designed computers based along the same lines as the human being.

Anything that will ever be invented has to be *imagined* beforehand; everything is in the creative process, and it starts in the mind. Everything is in the mind. That's all you have, and there is only love – that's what you are. You are a conscious reflection of your soul and of the God energy. I know I've gone on quite a bit about all of this but you know it's true.

You really do create your world.

We are all connected to the God energy and the Creator, so we are all part of that force; therefore, we are all in the creative process because God creates. He creates planets and universes at a rapid pace, constantly, so that your spirit and soul can visit and live, and you have a physical experience to grow as a spirit.

You are also part of that creative God process. Therefore, you are always creating something, either something good or something bad, or a mixture of both. We create all the time just as we create life and have children, so that the soul can come and experience physical life.

We are always creating.

You've only got to look around you to see this process of creation taking place. Look around you, at modern technology, telephones, cars and planes.

Spiritual Guides

I want to mention guides as well since we all have guides and no one walks on this earth alone.

We all have a team of spirits who walk beside us and the reason is that you have a life and, because of that, you need to be guided. We all need to be guided to meet the right people and to talk to the right people in our lives. If you're in the wrong relationship and spirit doesn't want you in it, because there's somebody else for you, they will always try and move you along.

Your guides are there to guide you, to help you.

You choose your guides in the spiritual realms and they come back here with you. It's funny, I always see it like, you sit round a table, you and your team. They're not your guides then, they're just colleagues in the realms of spirit.

You sit together and discuss your upcoming life now or maybe in five or eighty five years, (no time in Spirit). You choose to come back to this planet, back to earth or a different planet; you choose your guides - they come with you, they come around you and you experience life together.

Fascinatingly, it's likely that our guides come in at certain times when we need them. They'll come and help us in difficult situations in our lives and they'll guide us in certain areas.

When you're going through your worst times, you are helped the most but, of course, you are completely unaware of this. Have you ever wondered how you have managed to get through your darkest hours? Well, that's easy to answer; you are supported, guided and lifted through your darkest times.

They lead us on to different things and that's what guides are there to do; to help us and put us in situations where we need to be put to learn. It comes back to the whole thing where people say there is no such thing as coincidence and there isn't; you might have noticed. I've mentioned this a few times, but when people say you can choose your friends but not your family that is not true. All that is incorrect.

The likelihood is that you've chosen one another before. In a previous life, your brother may have been your dad; your aunt may have been your daughter.

They come to help you along; to guide you as the name states. Guides come to show you where you need to go and everyone has them and you'll feel them in many different ways. It always reminds me of the film *The Adjustment Bureau* with Matt Damon; there is so much going on that we are not aware of.

When I am working with my mediumship, I know my guides are there working with me. There is a whole team of them standing between me and spiritual realms, working out who is coming through. Your guides and helpers are working with you, helping you, instructing you and helping you grow in your life. Obviously, when you pass back to spirit, they are waiting for you as well.

Choosing Your Family

Also, going back to that old saying, 'you choose your friends but you can't choose your family.'

Well, that's not actually true. You do choose your family and you choose your friends.

You choose your family in the spiritual realms. Before you come here, you choose your parents to give you the best learning that you could possibly get while you're having a life. So, you choose your parents in spirit, so that you can grow in the best way here, and that's how it works.

You've always chosen your parents; you always will. If you're reading this book and you have kids, your children chose you as their parent before they came here. We make clear, conscious decisions in the world of spirit before we come here. We sit around a table with our friends and colleagues in spirit, mainly those who are going to be our guides. We choose those who are going to work with us. We make a conscious decision there about those who are going to help us here.

The whole thing is pre-constructed before we come. It's a bit like flat pack furniture; all we do is assemble it and put it together. We simply follow the instructions that are laid out and we build it, try and make the best out of this life while you're here. It always brings me back to that film that I mentioned before, with Matt Damon, called 'The Adjustment Bureau'. I don't know whether you have seen it or not but that's an interesting film, an interesting concept in that there's so much more going on that we don't realize using our five senses. There's so much going on around us that is beyond our conscious thought.

Psychic Abilities

What I will say, though, is that all human beings are psychic.

Being psychic is a natural ability in us all. In fact, we are all born with this psychic ability. I've said it before and it's true. It is something that we can all do.

The human being has become clever. We don't need the ability to be psychic because we have telephones, and we have satellites now. We've invented guns and we're able to look after ourselves in all kinds of different ways which causes us to lose the use of this ability to feel things before they happen.

Going back many centuries ago, we would have had this psychic ability to be able to protect ourselves from the animal kingdom. Intuition as it were. We would have known when something was preying on us, and if there was a lion or tiger prowling around, it would have been possible to sense that something wasn't right.

When somebody walks into the room behind you, it is possible to feel their energy even before you turn round to see them. This is your psychic ability working.

This same ability is in everyone and, with practice, by working with it, it is possible to bring it out in you. Then you can embrace and start to use this ability in your life. It does work and is with everybody, so, just because you might not be a medium, or work as a medium, you are most definitely a psychic.

You just don't yet realise that it is there waiting to be brought out.

It lies dormant in every single human being.

Everyone has psychic ability and, if they wish so, they can develop it.

Not everyone can be a medium unfortunately. Mediums are born to do the work they do, that's what mediums are. Mediums communicate with the spirit realm. Psychics work with earth energy and their own energy and intuition.

Mediums come to this world after the many lives led with many experiences and lots of knowledge of different lifetimes and different experiences to become a medium. That has always been the case. It is something you're bound to do; it's not something you inherit.

One Big University

What also amazes me is how we are all so blissfully unaware that all this is going on. We spend our lives going to work; moaning about the economy; trying to make a few quid; trying to build a business; trying to hold down a job; trying to stay in a relationship; trying to have a relationship; trying to have kids; trying not to have kids.

The human being is blissfully unaware that all this is just one big carefully orchestrated illusion. It has been put together so seamlessly that you can't see the joints, and this always amazes me.

When I actually stop and I think about it, we do seem to wander around in our lives thinking 'this is it'.

But, of course, you're just having a holiday and your spirit has come here into one big university.

This is a school and you've come in here to learn, to watch, to take on information and grow and that's what you've come for.

That is the truth. That is what it is and there's no doubt about that.

The fact of the matter is, that this school, this college, this place, is good for the time that it exists as it does.

One day this planet will burn out like many millions of other planets and galaxies have burnt out around the cosmos.

But that's okay, because God's constantly building them. Creating more 'big universities'.

The Hall
Of Records

Many books will tell you about the place which is called the Hall of Records. When you go back to the spiritual realms, you go back to the Hall of Records to lay out the life you have just lived. You can see every single small detail; everything you've experienced, from your birth to when you died. Everything is recorded. Everything is written down and you can see your whole life. It is fascinating to be able to virtually relive your entire experience including the good and the bad stuff; in fact, everything you've learnt from all your experience here.

But your soul doesn't just have memories from one life. It has multiple memories from multiple lives and at that point, when you're back in the Hall of Records, you can then access all your lives. When you're back in spirit, when you're complete and you're whole again, you can see all your lives; every single one you've ever had, right from when your spark of light was lit by God. This was the start of your awareness and then you had your first life, multiple ones thereafter, up to and including this life.

You can experience and see every detail, as well. You know, you could have been a King; a robber; a woman or a man. You could have died young or grown old. You could have had multiple different diseases and overcome them all. You could have been disabled, or anything that life may have given you.

Through the Hall of Records, and being in spirit, you can not only look through every life you've ever had, but you can look at it and you can live it. Spirit also has the unique ability to be able to time travel. Spirit sees our tomorrow today, that's clairvoyance. You can come back here and go to the pyramids if you wanted to. You can walk around the pyramids and view everything in different time periods. Of course it's not the same as having a life here, but you could go to the bottom of the ocean, find lost civilisations or see Atlantis. You could also see other planets, to look at their species and into their history.

Spirit can go anywhere and do anything, but in spirit your eyes are always on the prize and the prize is in being closer to the God figure;

being part of the God energy. Then you're able to experience what it's like to make worlds, to build universes, to do many different things. You experience what it's like to comprehend and conceive the species; oh, all sorts of wonderful and amazing stuff!

My Gift

How Spirit Works With Me

Now you'll want to know about how I experience/communicate with spirits and the spiritual realms and how spirit works through me. I am someone who is what's called a clairsentient and I am also a clairvoyant.

Now a clairsentient is someone who *feels* spirit; I can *sense* their energies around me. It is mental mediumship and I feel their energy, often they will give me that which took them to spirit. It could be a heart condition, or lung cancer, stomach cancer, poisoning of the blood and emphysema, all different types of things. With cancer, I get the sickness where they had it. I can usually tell if the cancer has spread as I feel it all through my body. With a heart attack, I get a sharp pain in my chest and feel a heavy weight, like I am pinned down.

Those symptoms come in and assault my senses. It occasionally makes me feel dizzy and it always makes me physically aware of what is going on in my own body.

All types of people come through with lots of different ailments; but I have to say, I don't like suicide - not because of the symptoms, although I do feel it; but because of the sadness for them and their family.

The reason they do that is to imprint their last physical memories of their life here on this planet.

I am also a clairvoyant, so I *see* spirits as well. Sometimes I see them really clearly and don't feel them so much; other times it's the other way around. It is different degrees of how these senses work and that's how I experience spiritual communication.

It's a bit like when you're watching a TV programme at home. I get flashes of images in my mind. I often see it like that; this is spirit working with me. This is mental mediumship, so they input their information into my mind as if they're my own thoughts.

The clairvoyance can sometimes be a bit startling as I am seeing every scar, wart or dent in their face so clearly, it's like looking in the mirror. I've experienced that a lot of times over the years.

It is a very difficult form of mediumship because you have to work out which are your thoughts and which are theirs. It's sometimes quite complicated though. Of course, the more you do it, the easier it becomes.

I am able to recognise what spirit is showing me. For example, rather than thinking that I've got a headache, I begin to realise that this is somebody that passed from this world with a brain tumour, a lesion, or a stroke and I know it's not my pain but it is a spirit's pain.

It works in different degrees really.

I am not normally clairaudient (hearing spirits talking verbally), although I have experienced clairaudience over the years and sometimes this happens with music. They will give a particular piece of music to somebody as evidence of whoever has passed, and they bring this music with them.

With the clairsentience, I've felt as though a spirit was standing inside me and as I opened my mouth, their words come out. At the same time, I often felt my mannerisms change, the way I moved would have been exactly the way they moved when they were here, alive in this physical realm.

I've worked on stage and people have said: 'My God, he would do exactly what you're doing; he used to move exactly the way you're moving; the way he moved his eyebrows, and his facial features is the way you're moving your features as well!'

Sometimes I smell alcohol, flowers, cigarettes, cigars etc. When I'm talking, I only talk to people. I don't like talking to dogs, flowers or cats. They don't seem to have much to say, well, not that I could understand them anyway.

Often, many mediums will suffer with depression or will have lots of heartache and suffer pain physically and certainly, emotionally. The reason that mediums suffer, seemingly a bit more (although all human beings suffer, and I don't want to belittle anyone's life) is because we need to understand to be effective with the work we do.

We have to understand what somebody is going through or what they've gone through because that's the learning process of a medium.

The spirits are in a completely different energy form in their existence. They don't have a physical body, they are metaphysical. You are a physical energy; and they are metaphysical, but they do obviously intertwine in all our lives.

When it comes to mediumship, it's either in you or it isn't.

Mediums have had many, many lives and their abilities are the result of a combination of all of those lives led.

As a medium who is working *with* Spirit - and some mediums say you work *for* spirit, but that's just not true. You work *together* - you become a *team* and the guides and those who come through are part of a team effort.

This requires everyone to work together, which is part of the learning that takes so long to develop and understand.

The whole process is very long and a great amount of patience is required to do this work; but if you are patient and if you are true to it, you work hard and get on with it, then spirit will reciprocate. They know those who want to work and those who are true to them and to each other, and they will always help you out.

I have never been let down. I've never done a demonstration where no one has come through.

But the reality, the true reality, is that they've never let me down and I love them dearly because that's where we're all from. We all come from love and love is all there is.

I have always had evidence of survival for people, and I've never been let down in the work I do as a medium because I've got complete faith in spirit. They won't let me down; they see the work that I do here. They want me to work with them and I want to work with them, too, so they wouldn't let me down and I know that for sure. Just as I try to never let them down also. It's very much a two-way thing.

I have heard some mediums say when they're backstage, or in a dressing room, that they get spirits coming to start working with them before they get on stage.

I didn't work like that but, in recent years, I've found my work is changing and they do come to me prior to going on stage.

Funnily enough we all work slightly differently and I am a medium who, when I get on stage with the audience, I know where I'm going and which particular area or person I'm drawn towards.

I am usually quite specific on where I'm going, but I think some mediums, and there's nothing wrong with this, it's just how they work with their gift, they'll stand on stage and they then start working with the spirits and giving off the information they are being given. Because they don't know who their message is for at that time, they will throw information out to the audience to see who can pick it up.

That is just how some mediums work.

It is not how I work.

I like to be directed and know where I'm going and that's how I've always done it since this is how I was taught. It's how I work and is something that is just with me and that's how I do it.

I prefer it that way.

There's one thing I do understand with my spiritual work and that is that I don't know it all. In fact, the more I do it, the more I realise I don't know that much at all and there is more to learn. There is so much more that we don't understand as a species as we really are kept in the dark. The truth is, there is so much going on around us all the time that we're just not aware of.

The human being looks but can't see; we hear but we don't listen; we touch but we don't feel.

The reality is that I'm still learning.

I am still growing.

I am still very much a child with all this and still very much an apprentice who has so much to learn.

To be honest with you, I don't want that to change. All the time that I'm growing and learning, my soul is constantly evolving. I like the idea of that. I think it's important and everything I've experienced in my life, everything I do, is fundamental to the work I do.

Mediums are also born into this world to do the work of mediums. You can't take someone and turn them into a medium. If it's not with them originally, if they're not born with it, then you can't produce it. If they haven't got the sensitivity to be able to do the work, then they are not born to work with spirit.

Spirit works with those who want to work with them, and spirit always supports me. I have had some demonstrations that are better than others, I'll grant that but, at the end of the day, I'm only human.

They work through me in different degrees and at different levels, dependant, I guess, on how I feel.

If I've had a row with someone, or if work has not gone well and I'm upset for whatever reason or I feel ill, then my demonstrations aren't going to be as good or as sharp as they could be.

If I feel very positive, upbeat and happy, they are clearer.

To be honest with you, there is no rule of thumb. I haven't found a consistent way of working because they work with me how best suits them to get their message over to their loved ones.

So, that's how I work with spirit.

My Guides

Morning Cloud

The first of my guides that I met was my Native American spiritual friend, Morning Cloud. If you remember, I first became aware of him at my tarot reading with good friend Peter.

I got to know him properly a little while later during a meditation session at one of Peter's development circles. He was dressed in traditional attire with light brown robes and a headdress adorned with colourful feathers.

Simon

Another of my guides is Simon. Although, that's not his actual name. He did tell me his name, but I found it too difficult to pronounce as he is a Chinese Mandarin man. I call him Simon and he seems happy with that name.

He stands tall, towering above most at an impressive 6'5".

I recall the first time I became aware of him. I was walking through Buckham Park one afternoon and I noticed a man to my right. He was wearing a beautiful hand-stitched silk cloak that was made of every single colour of the spectrum. It was astoundingly gorgeous! It was actually his cloak, flapping in the wind that caught my attention to begin with.

Simon is my 'demo guide', as he is usually the one who comes through when I do my platform demonstrations.

Doctor Feligrew

I want to talk about Doctor Feligrew.

I call him my 'healing guide', as he only seems to be around when I am practicing healing.

I remember years ago, when I first became a Reiki Master and I used to run healing circles, well, one evening, while I was doing some healing, I felt energy around me from somebody who got so close that I could actually hear him. He was a very well-spoken English gentleman. I would say he was in his fifties, and I was made aware that he was from the Victorian England era; a Victorian gentleman.

He wasn't a very big man, he stood at about 5' 8" tall. He had jet black hair with a moustache and a neatly trimmed beard and he wore glasses.

He went by the name of Dr Feligrew, a Victorian surgeon, and basically he used to work at the raw end of it, so he would do operations.

He talked to me and I listened to him whilst I was healing. He was telling me about himself and when he was doing his work. It was so barbaric as there were no anaesthetics in his day. They were working with basic tools to do surgery. They would take your leg off with no anaesthetics and get you as drunk as a lord, so you didn't really know what was going on.

He showed me his life and the gentleman that he was. He was really a kind man who tried to do his best for his own species, to help them, but of course, they were very different days.

He said he had to drink a lot of alcohol, and I could smell alcohol all around him. The reason was because he couldn't be too sober to do what he did because it would upset him too much, but he tried his best to help people.

When I started to work with my healing he used to come in all the time. He would talk to me, in a posh accent and using Victorian English, about what was wrong with the patient, and I've had the most startling things told to me about people.

There was this particular time, for instance, that one of my students was lying on the healing bed. As I put my hands on them, I instantly knew what was wrong with them because he, Dr Feligrew, would tell me what the problem was. He said there was a problem with the pancreas and he went on describe it and then he showed me. It was truly amazing, as I could feel his hands through mine, almost as if he was working on them or through them.

I have told people things that only they and their consultants would have known. I don't know how you can do that, but it was him, Dr Feligrew, it wasn't me. It was him telling me and giving advice in terms of how to heal and what they needed to do.

As I talk about this now, it makes me feel I like I would like to do more healing, firstly because I feel that it could be good for people and it's good for me as well. Secondly, as I mentioned before, Dr Feligrew only seems to come through when I am practicing healing. He was a wonderful man; a very gentle and skilled surgeon.

You know what?
All human beings can heal, it's your birth right.

Zulu Warrior

I do have one guide who is a Zulu warrior.

One day when I was decorating a lady's house, I was looking out of the window, day dreaming (I've done a lot of that over the years) and he appeared, looked straight at me and he was smiling. As soon as I looked away, though, he had gone.

Past Lives

One of my favourite subjects is past lives.

There are some mediums that don't believe in past lives. I don't understand that, as the need for many lives is required for the evolvement of the soul. I've personally seen so many of them; I've been backwards and forwards here to this physical plane more times than a ping-pong ball.

Eton

It was back when I was in the house in Ifield, with my office behind the garage, and I was playing some relaxing music on the PC for my meditation. As I meditated and relaxed I saw a teacher coming in who was wearing a black gown and a teacher's hat, and it was quite clear this was going back quite a few hundred years.

I had a conversation with this man and I've never forgotten it to this day as it was the clearest and most bizarre conversation ever. He said that he taught me when I was at school at Eton, and that I was an Eton boy. He really liked me and had a real connection with me. I found this man's energy very gentle and compassionate.

I was fully conscious with my eyes closed but I spoke to him in my mind.

"Can you tell me about the life I had and who I was?" I asked him.

"No, I can't, because I'm not allowed. All I can tell you is to go ahead and enjoy the life you've got now because this is the most important one," he replied.

I have to say I was gutted. I wanted to know more; who I was; what was I like; so many questions but no answers. He'd captured my imagination and yet again I was hooked. I believe he was sent by the spirit realm to instigate my interest in reincarnation.

Not long after that, a friend of my Wife died of breast cancer and we went to her funeral, which was held in the church in the village in Ifield. I've told this story many times, although I'm sure nobody believes me.

I was standing in the church and I started to sing a hymn. For some reason that I couldn't explain, I recognised the words. As I was singing along, I looked down at my clothes and they had all changed. I no longer had the black suit on that I was wearing before. Now, I had on a black gown, which I realised was a school gown. As I looked around, I could see choirboys standing around the church. They were all singing and it became very apparent that I was no longer standing in the same church, but I was actually a school boy and found myself in the church at Eton College. It was the most bizarre thing to say the least and I remember thinking how incredible it all was. This isn't the sort of thing that happens; it was as if I had slipped into another dimension.

I was amazed and blown away by what I had just experienced. It seemed like a dream but I knew there was more to it than that. When I got home, I went onto my PC - the one I built (it was still working! That's also amazing!) and I pulled up the Eton College website.

They had a web cam at the time that followed the Cloisters covered-walkway and although I'd never seen Eton College in my life before, as I scanned with the web cam, I knew what was coming around the next corner! There was a massive board with some boys names on it but I knew this was coming and actually said to my wife that it was there, exactly as I'd seen it before.

I knew I'd lived that life. I had been an Eton boy and I had studied at Eton College. From the feelings I experienced, I knew that I had loved it there.

So strong were those feelings, that I have, in fact, been able to visit the school and take a walk around. You don't get to see much but I didn't need to; it just all felt so right. The strange thing is, I stood outside the college, right on the corner of Keates Lane (the poet Keates went to Eton) and felt lost in that moment. All my surroundings became strangely familiar as my focus of attention changed, the essence of that life I once had, started to come back.

A Member of The Aristocracy

I've always known that I have been here before. There are some things in life you just know. From a young boy, I have had this massive interest in mansion houses of the British aristocracy, their homes and the way they used to live. A bit of a strange interest for a young boy you might think, but these stately homes draw me like a magnet.

I have always had a fascination for grand estates, and I could never work out why; but the whole jigsaw fitted together when, a few years back, I realised that I had had a life as part of the aristocracy. I was a country gent, and I lived in a mansion, although I don't think that I was a particularly nice man in those days. Actually, I think I was a bit of a bastard (excuse the swearing). It feels so right when I am around these buildings. Although I wasn't very nice, I enjoyed the privileges of such a life.

Nevertheless, I had that life once and that is why today I have this fascination for the gentry and for mansion houses. If I see a big house, I can't help myself. I go up the drive to have a look. I absolutely love them. I also have a very strange interest in snooker as well, although I could never work out why that was either. I now realise that I had a billiard room in my country estate where I used to play and I still love the game today. I still play but not very well I have to say.

I'll never forget, when I was a lad, my dad took me to a working men's club and they had a snooker room there. My heart just melted. Seeing the snooker tables ignited a memory in me as a young boy that I could not explain.

What happens to you is that the memories of your past lives filter through to this life. Certainly some of the nice ones, but also some of the horrible ones as well. That must be why I have a great interest in mansion houses, in snooker and everything to do with the aristocracy because that was one of my significant past lives; part of my history within this world. I would love to relive that life but alas, no. This is it for me now - this is the main event. You cannot relive, in its entirety, a past life. All you can get are glimpses and feelings.

Could you imagine me turning up at one of these stately homes and declaring it as mine because 300 years ago it was? Straight back to the psychiatrist I would go. Even if I did find it, no one would ever believe me. Why should they?

That life has made a big impression on my soul, so much so that I carried some of those memories and visions back into this life.

Slavery
There have been so many different lives that I've remembered over the years. One time I saw myself as a young black man. I will never forget - I was in this meditation, and had gone into a very deep state, and as this life appeared to me, I could see myself standing on a sandy beach in the blazing sun.

It was a lovely, hot day and the water was crystal clear as it lapped at my feet and I was with a young woman. I presume this was my wife because there was such love between us, which was the most wonderful feeling ever.

I remember looking out over the ocean and seeing a huge galleon ship which was far out at sea and there were three or four rowing boats coming ashore. It wasn't just me and my wife there, there were ten or fifteen of us on this beach. I remember a feeling of excitement as I watched them getting closer. I felt we were there to welcome them to our home.

But then the sailors grabbed all of us men, they left the women and they dragged us to the rowing boats and took us onto the ship.

I remember seeing myself being manacled where I sat with a massive oar in my hand and I was made to row. Throughout this part of the meditation, I felt so much sadness. Something happened to the boat and, as the boat sank, I remember seeing myself struggling to release the chains which held me by my wrists and ankles.

I couldn't release myself and I watched my life pass away in that boat and, as it did, I felt my energy leave and go up and out and then I came back from the meditation.

Farmer's Wife

I have been part of the aristocracy, an Eton Boy and a black slave. However, I also remember I was once a farmer's wife. I'll always fondly recall this one because it was beautiful. I was in a farmhouse, and I was a larger than life lady, built for comfort, not for speed. I remember laying in the bed. It was my last moment on this planet, in this life. I had borne three healthy strong sons and they all stood around my bed. They were crying and holding my hand as I slipped away and that was a lovely peaceful passing for me.

This was a wonderful experience and then I went home back to the spiritual realm.

It is hard to get your head round the realisation that you've lived other lives as well as this one, but it's true. You don't realise until you go home, back to the spirit realm, where you lay all your lives out ahead of you and you see what you've done. You're not allowed to experience all of your memories here but it's possible to link in to a few. When you're born, your memory is wiped clean for good reason, otherwise it would effect this life too much and your focus would be taken away from the most important life - this one. The life you have right now.

I run many teaching groups and I've been able to help people look at their past lives and who they were and to experience it in a very deep way. It's actually helped them in this life now because it releases some of the pain they are still carrying. They didn't realise why they had these pains and these thoughts until they'd seen into their past lives. What they found helped them here in the present. It is fascinating but that's something else I've done for a very long time.

There you go, all these different experiences I've had and more will come out as I think about them.

Enlightened Life

Houses And Ghosts

Going back to the house in Ifield, as I mentioned, it was like Piccadilly Circus in there with all the spiritual energies flowing constantly through. However, I was now realising that I was in the house for a reason. As I started to develop spiritually, I realised that I was not on my own in that house. I say 'I', as, although we lived together as man and wife, it is my own experiences that I am talking about.

I slowly improved the property in my own time as I could do a lot of the work myself and that saved a few quid. But as I worked, I became more and more aware that there were spirits around me, listening to me and watching what was going on.

I remember one particular day when I was in my office, I was working from home doing quotes and general paperwork and I turned the computer on and loaded the word processing package. I went downstairs and made myself a cup of tea. When I went back into the room, I could feel energy. I looked at the computer and the whole computer screen was full of words. Somebody had been in there typing, but that was impossible. I was the only one at home. My wife was at work, the house was quiet; well, that's what I thought - how wrong can you be?

Goodness knows how they had managed to do that, but this shows you the amount of energy that was in that house. The whole screen was full of words; some of it was jumbled, however, there were lots of references to God, and to spirit and other stuff that I can't remember now. In hindsight, I should have printed it off. But at the time, I panicked and deleted the whole page, which was quite stupid, but I was rather scared to say the least. Let's face it, it's not every day your computer starts typing by itself. I know it's difficult to believe, but it really did happen. The energy in that house was so strong that someone took the opportunity to use it and have a play.

I've never forgotten that. It was amazing to me but also quite scary. It just proves that you're not alone in a house, even though you think you are.

Going Pro

I had been doing my healing circle for quite some months, when I was approached and asked to do a tarot reading. Soon, someone else asked me to do a psychic reading. Pretty soon, I was being asked on a regular basis to see if I could connect with anyone from the spiritual realms, in one way or another.

So, it was then that I decided to become a professional medium and charge for my services and time. I kind of fell into it really.

During the day, I worked at my business, and then, two or three evening a week and the odd weekend, I would do readings for people.

Working as a professional medium, I have had some very interesting readings over the years and you just can't question some of the experiences, or the readings, because they have been so accurate. Some of them have made my jaw drop open in astonishment to be honest.

As I have been doing this for very many years now, I have done a lot of readings, too many to recount. However, I have dedicated a whole section further on in this book to some of my most memorable readings and experiences.

My First Demonstration

I had been doing tarot readings and personal psychic readings to one or two people at a time for a little while, when I was approached by a friend that I had done some Reiki training with. She ran the Three Bridges Spiritualist Church and she wanted me to do a demonstration of mediumship to an audience (this is also called a 'platform demonstration').

Well, I had never done anything like this before, although by now I had been to many demonstrations run by other mediums.

I was nervous, but I agreed.

On the night, a coach load of Dutch people arrived. Yes, they had hired a coach and driven all the way from Holland just to see me. Before we began, not only do I notice that none of those who had arrived from overseas spoke any English, but they had brought an interpreter with them. Then, to my shock, I noticed a priest within the crowd too.

I started the demonstration and as soon I spoke, the interpreter spoke to translate what I was saying and then the priest began to pray, out loud. I tried to speak a little louder and so did the interpreter, then so did the priest!

It was like a comedy show gone wrong!

You really couldn't make it up!

Needless to say, it was not what I would consider a 'successful' first experience at a platform demonstration. Thankfully, it didn't put me off trying again, but it very nearly did!

What Happens At My Demonstrations?

Not many people have been to a demonstration of mediumship before. But it's just like a theatre/auditorium or large room or spiritualist church, and someone like me, a medium, on a small platform or stage. Sometimes, there may be ten or fifteen people in the audience, at other times, there could be over a hundred.

The thing is, I never know who is going to come through in spirit. And I never know who the message is going to be for until I have tapped into those energies.

Each and every demonstration that I have ever done has always been different. I've always had different experiences.

So, when I begin my demonstration, I link in with the spiritual realm and soon numerous spirits will be coming through with their own realities that I then begin working with.

I am then directed to an area, often drawn to the exact person I should be with, to whom I need to connect with.

Mostly, I don't know why, but there is always a reason for a clairvoyant message; information spirit gives me that is personal to the receiver.

Usually, I then start feeling the symptoms of how someone has passed (clairsentience), and then give validation of who it was. It doesn't always work like this, but it seems to be the way I work.

I put out the message of the symptoms I'm feeling at someone's point of death, the spirit of the person who passed, and is now communicating with me. I tell the audience exactly what I am feeling and how I think this person passed back to the spiritual realms.

I then put out a message to the receiver, again, telling the audience something personal that spirit has told me, to help validate a connection. Often, at this point, someone in the audience will recognise their loved one trying to communicate.

Let me give you a few examples of a demonstration:

The Husband And The Mother

"Who was the gentleman," I asked, "who passed with emphysema? I ask this because he is knocking the back of my legs and saying, 'oi, mate!'. And he's telling me how much he hated having to have the oxygen mask. He said he couldn't do this anymore and he just gave up which was a big contrast with how he was in life."

I connected with a lady in the audience. She needed this message, and I felt the atmosphere and the energy between them.

"He's very much around you," I said, "and he says you're running yourself ragged and not eating properly, is that true?" She didn't need to answer as I already knew that she hadn't been eating properly. *I could feel it.*

Since I'm clairsentient and clairvoyant (which means I can feel and see things), I can also sense the energy of the person who is receiving the messages.

"I'm feeling very busy with you and I just can't sit down," I tell the lady who wasn't eating properly.

It turns out, the spirit making contact with her through me was her husband. I then go on to tell her more about him.

"He was a party man, very sociable and he didn't like to be alone. He didn't want to give up smoking. He knows he should have done but it just caught up with him in the end."

I also mentioned to her about moving house as I could see her looking at another property in another area.

"I can feel someone coming through, who passed with a stomach cancer," I said. "They're giving me enough pain in my own stomach to make sure I know what they're trying to tell me. This lady didn't want to be a burden, and she tried not to put pressure on anyone else. She handed roses to someone to say 'thank you' to them for looking after her. She'd love you to light a candle on her birthday."

Then the woman spirit who was making contact with me stepped back a bit and apologised for making me feel her suffering. But that's my job; that's what I'm here to do.

It was the woman's mother who had now come through. She showed me a drawer which she pulled out. She asked for her daughter to go and check it because she'll find something there which she doesn't want anyone else to see.

"Your Mother is fine now," I said to the woman, "but she's asking you to always think of her at Christmas and she says, 'I'll always be there'. Your Mum tells me that she had a bit of trouble with her feet, but they're fine now."

At the end of the message I always pass on their love from spirit before I break the connection. To break that connection, I generally have a drink of water. This momentarily helps close the link to the spiritual realms.

The Ship

A woman once asked me: "What happens when you die?"

"You stop breathing," was my very detailed and scientific answer.

As well as bringing in laughter, I also want to help everyone to understand that you don't ever die and that your energy goes on indefinitely. It is merely your physical body that ceases to exist. Not your soul, or your energy, your spirit.

Sometimes spirits just pick on me and won't let me move on, but they come through as they want to do. It's not up to me and in one of my demonstrations, this great big boat came right into the room. I could see this enormous ship sail into the hall where I was working. I could see the funnels smoking and the bow of the ship and even people walking along the deck.

As soon as I saw the ship, I felt a pain in my head and asked a woman if her husband had had anything wrong with his head?

"No," she replied, "nothing wrong with his head, but he did go a bit doo lally at the end!" (Something wrong with his head then!).

The Grandparents

One day, a grandmother energy came through. I feel a female energy and I know it will be mother, grandmother or great-grandmother. I then get a sense of who it is. I can feel that I can't get oxygen in my lungs quickly enough. I feel this in my chest, in my breathing, like an emphysema or lung cancer. Both these symptoms feel the same to me as a medium.

I can feel that my hair is white with this lady, and I feel pain in my feet. She tells me she had trouble with her feet but, she tells me: 'They're fine now.' As I've mentioned before, everything is repaired in spirit.

I then feel a grandfather energy. Similarly, I get a male energy and sense who this is. I felt as though I had a moustache and I'm in the military. This man comes in and he barges into me. I can feel him pushing me to the side and he is lively, active and strong.

I really like this man's energy.

He tells me he didn't believe in any of this but now he knows he's got it all wrong! Then I feel myself being taken abroad, somewhere hot, that's where I find myself.

Often, I will get the name of the person that has passed and I'm able to give that as validation of survival evidence.

Having Fun

There have been many demonstrations over the years and when spirits come through, if they had a good sense of humour when they were alive, they bring that through from the spiritual realms. They still have happiness with them when they're home.

I do work with a lot of laughter and with a bit of sarcasm, I can't help it. It's all done tongue in cheek and there's no harm in it. When spirits come through and there has been a lot of laughter in their lives, they bring that laughter through. It just makes for a wonderful demonstration when you have that.

Spirits want us to laugh and have fun. The last thing they want us to do is to feel sad and upset. They want to see us happy and making the most of our lives.

In a demonstration of mediumship, they don't want to see us cry. They're in a place that is so beautiful; there's no pain; they never get tired or hungry; they can go anywhere they want. Time doesn't exist and it's a beautiful reality that we can't even begin to imagine here. So, the last thing they want to see you do when they come through is to be upset. They'd much sooner see you laughing.

Spirit can come through with a lot of humour as well. When I'm working, I have had the likes of Morecambe and Wise, Les Dawson and other British comedians come through. Some of them have been passed for a few years now, but I think they've been watching me, and I have a bit of a link with them and so, that's good.

I enjoy working with an audience and bringing messages through from the spirit realms. Hopefully people who listen to me enjoy the way I work. I can't for the life of me be too serious; that's not me. I've tried, but just can't. I love the laughter and so do spirit. It raises the energy. It uplifts people. I guess it's a kind of healing and, as they say, laughter is the best medicine.

Becoming A Dad

We did the house up over the years and my business started to grow. In the early 90's, my Wife announced that we were expecting our first child. I was in my early thirties by now and more than ready to start a family.

As most expectant fathers, I was filled with a mixture of emotions. I was happy and excited that I was going to be a father for the first time, but I was also worried and apprehensive. A child was a lot of responsibility. I knew I was more than capable of taking on such a role, but I couldn't help but feel slightly anxious. Still, my elation and excitement far surpassed my feelings of concern.

In 2003 we had our first child, Emily Jayne, a pretty little girl. My Wife and I were overjoyed! She was a beautiful bundle of joy.

That's when I lost my office. Well, she had to have somewhere to sleep, and we couldn't put her under the stairs like Harry Potter now, could we? We had an attached garage on the side and we cut it in half so the back of the garage formed into an office. It was quite good. I was away from the house and had my own space.

We made a desk out of the worktop which went all the way around the room. I remember one day, I had to do some paperwork. First off, I made myself a cup of tea. I do like a cup of tea, you might have noticed! As I went towards the office, I looked through the window and I could see the long desk and there were people sitting on it!

There they were, almost as a physical incarnation of their spirit and I could see them talking to one another. There was a woman and a couple of blokes, but then they stopped talking and just stared at me.

Then I heard the woman saying, "My word, he can see us."

Then they just disappeared and that was really very odd, but by now I think I was getting more used to it, odd happenings. I wasn't as scared. Okay, that's a porky pie! I was still scared really, but I tried to convince myself I wasn't.

About two years later we had another beautiful little girl, Jessica Jayne, and she is totally different to Emily. They say you never get two the same!

Magical House

Anyway, let's get back to the house in Ifield.

We had been living there many years by this time.

This was a kind of magical place, and I am almost tempted to go back and buy it again because it was so wonderful, although I didn't think so at the time.

I recall getting up in the middle of the night to do the night feed. I was knackered, just as all parents are with little ones. I was becoming more and more aware of spirits and spiritual energy by this time. I remember sitting in the lounge with Emily on my knee and a full bottle of milk in her mouth and I turned the telly on to keep me awake as I was absolutely exhausted. I am sure many parents out there use the same tactic!

The first programme that came on was a documentary on the Native Americans and how they lived. I couldn't turn that programme off. It captivated me and held me, and I was literally glued to the television. I carried on watching for most of the night because it interested me so much. As you now know, I do have a Native American guide who has been with me since I started this work, Morning Cloud.

I worked hard when I was in the building industry and was often exhausted but I remember going to bed one night. We had Emily in her cot, and I remember being woken up and feeling someone in the room. So I sat up in front of our bed where there was a bank of mirrored wardrobes. As I looked, I could see the reflection of a man standing in the doorway of the bedroom.

I turned round and sure enough there was a man just standing there. I think he was in a suit, but he was standing there just looking at me. Despite being tired, I knew it was a spirit. I was now used to them, so I knew it wasn't somebody who had broken in or entered the house. But, being so exhausted, I simply turned over in bed and went back to sleep. Now, that's mad don't you think? But at this point, it really didn't bother me as I knew it was a spirit.

Goodbye Dad

I remember when Emily was probably around five years old, and Jessica was two and my Father had been really ill. We had all been away on holiday to Fuerteventura for two weeks and, as I walked along the beach one night with my family, I felt my guide, Morning Cloud, around me. He said to me that my Dad was very poorly and that the time was coming for him to go home, back to the spiritual realm.

When we got home, sure enough my Dad had been taken into hospital. I jumped in my car and paid a visit to Chesterfield to see him. I knew his time was coming as my guide had said so. When I saw Dad, he told me that he knew he was going to pass, but that he wasn't scared; he was tired and had had enough of his time here. He was a lovely man and I was so close to my Dad and I miss him so much. I think I always will, but I know that one day I will see him again. I know he knows that I love him and I feel him around from time to time.

When my Father died, I had received a phone call from my brother to say he had passed. It was a sad day and one that will be etched in my mind forever.

I had walked from the hall where the phone was and into the kitchen. As I walked in, Emily was sitting on one of the bar stools. She looked at me and bless her, she didn't know that her Granddad was ill, not at five years old, and she said, "Daddy, why is Granddad standing behind you? I can see Granddad and he has his hand on your shoulder."

I didn't need it, but she gave me clear evidence that my father had passed. By this time, he was fully aware of the work I was doing with Spirit, although I don't think he was too happy about it, he accepted it.

After my Dad left the physical realm, I could feel him around me, which was particularly upsetting for me as my Dad became my friend not just my Father. As I got older and matured, I saw him for the man he was rather than just my Dad. He didn't have an enemy in the world and was a real character. So, yes, my Dad passed and my Emily could see him around me and I could feel him near me from time to time too.

I do miss him dearly.

He was proud of me, I know, but I didn't find out until he died. My auntie told me that he did nothing but talk about me. I miss him so much and I didn't think I would but, as I grew into a man, I realised what he meant to me.

He used to say to me as a boy, 'you can't put an old head on young shoulders'. I never understood as a kid, but I do now.

My Mum lived on for several years after my Dad had passed. But once she also left this earthly plane, I could also sense her close to me occasionally.

An Expensive Lesson

Eventually, we moved out of that house. We were looking for another property to buy and every house we seemed to look at had a ghost in it because, by then, my awareness had grown to such an extent that I could actually feel them around me, very close to me.

I remember we looked at a big four-bedroom house in Crawley, which was going cheap as the people just wanted to sell it and emigrate to Canada.

This was a lovely house but it needed a bit of work doing to it. The first thing that I became aware of as we walked through the front door was that there was a ghost in there, a spirit who was stuck. This was a young lad who had passed on and I found out later that the tragedy for the family was that it was their son. To try and get over their tragedy and reconcile themselves, the grieving family had decided to emigrate.

The house was up for quite a cheap price and we probably should have bought it. I think we were actually meant to have it. I know that now, looking back, but unfortunately, we didn't buy it.

We decided not to move out from Ifield until an opportunity for a bit of land came up, and when it did, I seized it with both hands. It had always been my dream to build my own place, our family home, from the foundations to the roof, and finally it looked like I was going to achieve it. Man, I cannot begin to tell you how excited I was.

We ended up moving into my Mother-in-Law's house for nearly a year while I sorted out the land. Unfortunately, the man I was buying the land from decided to use the planning permission that I had paid for and all the work I had done on the land, and build it for himself; for his own greedy profit.

We ended up homeless. My ambitions, the dreams of our family home and our future were gone, vanished into thin air.

I am a spiritual man and live and let live, I say, but I can tell you, what I wanted to do to him I can't write. I was angry beyond words. My Wife nearly had a breakdown and we were homeless. He had led me on, getting me to spend my money on planning and the like, promising to sign over the land on a weekly basis. We sold our house to raise the money to buy it. We sold because he said he wanted the money straight away. I took him at his word, I trusted him.

I learnt a valued lesson. An expensive lesson.

Back On Our Feet

Thankfully, good fortune came my way, and we found a house in Crawley. This was a detached house which also needed a lot of work doing to it (there's a theme *building* here, pun intended!).

And, true to form, when I got this house there was the ghost of the lady who had lived there before. She lived there before the people we had bought it from but when she died, she passed away in one of the upstairs bedrooms; my daughter Emily's bedroom actually and she was trapped.

All mediums learn the ability to rescue and help home those who are stuck here on the earth plane, so I freed the spirit of this woman and sent her home.

Time moved on and my business became reasonably successful. Eventually, we had saved enough money to put a deposit down on another property that we wanted to rent out. This would mean equity as a pension for us in the future.

And guess what? As usual, this house, when we went to look at it, had a ghost and this was actually the gentleman who owned it before we did.

He had died at home and his spirit was still in the house. I viewed it and realised this immediately, so I went back to my vehicle and I was able to set his spirit free. You don't have to be in the same space as the spirit - you can help them from anywhere.

That is exactly what I did. I sat alone in my car and meditated, 'tuning in' as it were, to the spiritual realms. He didn't actually want to leave, and I was chasing him around all over the house. I don't know why he didn't want to go but eventually the metaphysical door opened and my guides helped him on.

I actually heard his wife say, "it's about time you came back here." I think she had been waiting for him for a long time. That experience was a bit strange. I remember turning the radio on just after I did it and they were playing 'Unchained Melody' which is featured in the film 'Ghost'.

It turns out that just about every house I've gone to buy, and every house I've moved to has always had a ghost in it. So, they have kind of followed me around, I suppose. But you know, I'm so used to it now that it doesn't bother me at all. I don't even think about it as being bizarre since this is all normal to me. It's what I do.

Helpless

When Emily was around eight years old, she began to experience frequent headaches with bouts of nausea and vomiting. On many occasions, my Wife and I took her to the doctors. Unfortunately, after many tests, Emily was misdiagnosed. My Wife and I just couldn't get our heads round it. What on earth was wrong with our poor daughter? We knew our baby girl, we knew something was wrong, something seriously wrong. But yet we didn't seem to be getting any answers that made sense.

 We eventually went private in the hopes of getting some answers for our sick child. The doctor, Emily's personal consultant, was fantastic. He was very attentive and professional and assured us he would do all he could for our daughter. He even gave us his personal mobile phone number, should we have any concerns or worries at all. He gave us hope where there had been almost none.

While waiting for the results of ever more tests through the private medical clinic, Emily seemed to deteriorate further. She was still suffering from excruciating headaches and the vomiting had not eased. She was losing weight, eating little, sleepy, with very little energy when she was awake, and even lacked interest in the things she usually enjoyed doing. It was heart-breaking to see. Our eldest daughter seemed a shadow of her former self. And it all seemed to be happening so quickly.

I cannot tell you how utterly helpless I felt. I am her dad, her protector. And I could do nothing for her. I wanted to help my little girl get better so badly, but all I could offer was love and hugs, and it didn't seem enough. I felt like inside, I was constantly screaming out for help.

Then, one Saturday, Emily took a turn for the worst. We called her consultant on his personal number and he asked us to take her to A&E at Crawley Hospital and said that he would meet us there. We done as we were asked and when we arrived, Emily had a head CT scan, which showed that she had a brain tumour at the back of her head. The staff in A&E arranged for a blue light ambulance to get us to Atkinson Morley Hospital where Emily then underwent brain surgery for ten hours in the hopes of removing the tumour.

The surgery was a success!

They had managed to remove the offending tumour and would now send it off for testing. Our joy was short lived, as, when the test results returned, it showed the tumour to be malignant. Our Emily would need to have more treatment and they didn't know how long for at this stage.

The next eighteen months or so were incredibly difficult for us all, especially Emily, our little fighter. She spent most of those months in hospital receiving chemotherapy and then radiotherapy. She continued to lose weight and looked painfully thin and pale. Her hair all fell out due to the treatment, which is truly gut wrenching for any little girl to have to go through. We assured her that she was still beautiful and that her hair would grow back once she was all better from the cancer.

It was hard for my Wife and I, not being able to be with Emily all the time when she was in hospital. We still had Jessica to look after and to get to school, and I still had a business to run and bills to pay. We were lucky to have the help of my Mother-in-Law too, as she would frequently help with Jessica and school runs.

Often I would find it difficult to concentrate at work as my mind would keep wandering back to Emily and her illness, wondering if she was ever going to get better.

I found myself praying, asking my guides and spirit to help my daughter, but there's only so much they can do for us here. I knew that, but it didn't stop me from asking anyway.

That feeling of helplessness shrouded me often in those times.

A Ray Of Hope

One afternoon, we took Emily to see her consultant.

"It's good news, Emily!" he said with a beaming smile. "You no longer need to have treatment. The cancer is gone."

I cannot even begin to tell you the relief that I felt upon hearing those words. Our Emily, our strong little fighter, had overcome cancer. She would need to have regular MRI scans, to make sure that the cancer didn't return. But she no longer needed invasion treatment. She was cancer free!

Unfortunately, I felt like her Mother and I had lied to her. We told her and assured her that her hair would grow back. It never did. But do you know what? She bravely and proudly shows her bald head for all to see. She does not wear head scarfs, hats or wigs. No. Emily shows her head for all to see, as, in her own words 'it's part of who I am'. I am so proud of her.

The South Coulsdon Golf Club heard about our Emily's illness and they wanted to do something special for her and us as a family. They were a great community there and they often raised money for their own charity and our Emily became something of a patron or mascot for them.

Once Emily was well, we were presented with a family holiday to Florida, to help us make some good memories after all the heartache we had endured when Emily was ill. It was all paid for! The flights, the hotel and even the theme park tickets! It was truly incredible to be given such a gift.

The holiday was amazing! Emily and Jessica loved every second that we were there.

But I think that is when I first noticed a distance growing between my Wife and I.

I couldn't help but think back to what Emily's consultant had once said to my Wife and I, when Emily first started her cancer treatment.

"Unfortunately, the statistics show that 88% of couples who have a child with cancer end up divorcing."

I kind of understood it. As hard as it was to admit, life had been really tough for my Wife and I, as parents of a desperately sick child. It was traumatic, for us almost as much as it was for our Emily. The helplessness, the pain of watching our daughter suffer and there being absolutely nothing at all that we could do to help. Yet, we still had to contend with the normal pressures of life that every person and couple face.

I just hoped that we still had a chance to save our marriage.

My Diagnosis

In 2003, I was at work renovating a property. I was fitting some cornice and pelmets in a kitchen, just doing some finishing touches. I remember feeling quite ill. Just so unwell.

I packed up work for the day and headed home. I felt worse than I had ever felt in my entire life. I got home and just slumped in a chair. I don't remember getting to bed, but the next morning, I felt even worse.

I began to notice a numbness creeping over the right side of my body, starting with my hand and arm. Gradually, over the next twenty-four hours or so, the numbness took over the whole of my right side.

I was extremely worried. Was I seriously ill?

I went to the doctor and was referred for an MRI scan a few weeks later.

Unfortunately, the scan showed some white patches on my spinal cord. I was diagnosed with Multiple Sclerosis.

It was hard for me to take at first. What did this mean? Would I get feeling back in the right side of my body? Would I still be able to work?

I was very poorly and not able to do very much.

It didn't help that, I could still feel an ever-growing distance between my Wife and I. I felt like I had become a burden on her, with my illness. We were hardly ever intimate anymore. We were spending less time together and often batted heads over the littlest of things.

Over the next few months, I gained back some feeling in my body and, thankfully, I was able to continue working.

An Unexpected Opportunity

By 2013, my health had improved somewhat, but my marriage hadn't.

If anything, it seemed to be going in the opposite direction. Not only were we becoming increasingly distant, but now I was sleeping downstairs on the sofa and no longer in the marital bed that we had shared for the best part of twenty years. We were rowing almost every day. I was avoiding going home, throwing myself into my spiritual work more, anything to keep me away.

Then, one night, we argued so badly. In no uncertain terms, she told me to leave. I wasn't sure if she meant permanently or just for a short while, but I upped and left and went to a nearby café.

I called a friend of mine who was, at that time, living and working in the United States of America. I practically cried to her down the phone. I was at my lowest ebb. I still wasn't feeling great health wise, and now my marriage was on the verge of collapsing.

I was lost.

I was low.

"Come to America!" said my friend.

And so, I did.

America, Here I come!

Just a few weeks later, I found myself on a plane to Los Angeles. My Wife wasn't what you'd call 'excited' about it, but we needed a break from each other. I had only planned on a two-week trip, which would have given us ample time away from one another.

I spent some time with my friend who had invited me and, of course, I did the whole Hollywood thing. How can you go to Los Angeles and not go to Hollywood? I rented a nice car and drove up to Bel Air to view my next mansion I'd like to buy!

What a magical place! The playground of the rich, so they say. I found the whole American experience delightful. I was welcome with open arms and felt very at home there.

I was mistaken for the British actor, Vinnie Jones, twice; once in the local shopping mall and the other by a hotel waitress who was asking for my autograph.

While I was in LA, I met a lady from the Healing Light Sanctuary.

Anyway, I was invited to take part in a radio show that the sanctuary were doing. The radio show I carried out was streamlined live across the world. I found this a very strange experience as I was in my hotel bedroom on the telephone. I felt strangely nervous and uneasy as there was no audience to interact with, just me and the mirror. This interview is readily available on YouTube under the title of 'Jamillah A Shabazz Interview - Nigel Gaff'.

The radio interview was about me and the work I do as a medium. This was my first radio interview. As the interview progressed, we covered many things that I've spoken about in this book. We had a few callers asking questions and I found the whole experience very different but interesting as I'm used to a live audience.

A few days later, I was invited to take part in a TV Show. I attended the Afro Caribbean Spiritualist Church in Downtown LA where I performed a demonstration of my mediumship to an audience of around forty people. I gave several messages to members of the audience from relatives and loved ones who had passed from here back to the spirit realms. It was all recorded for a television show. It was totally different to the radio show that I took part in without a live audience in front of me.

I loved the USA and the American attitude toward spiritualism; certainly, in the state of California, they seem to be more open to this way of life.

I couldn't quite believe that I was able to do my spirit work across the Atlantic. It made me consider working there one day, to return and to continue my spiritual career in the USA.

Broken

On my return from Los Angeles, I found that the time apart from my Wife had done nothing to help improve our relationship. If anything, it seemed to have made it worse. I wasn't sure what we could do anymore to save our marriage.

In March 2014, I came to the decision, for the sake of all of us, both my Wife, my daughters and myself, to leave. Permanently. It wasn't a decision I had made lightly. It was months, if not years, of arguing, sleeping on the sofa, avoiding going home and feeling like I wasn't wanted around, all built up to the point that, I knew that there was no way back for us.

It wasn't fair on my Wife and I to be stuck in a loveless marriage, or for our girls to constantly witness our bickering and the negative energies between us. It wasn't fair and it wasn't healthy. And I knew that.

So, I left.

I rented a small apartment for three months while waiting for the tenant who was currently living in our property in Northgate (we had bought the property as a pension investment a few years back), to vacate. Only he didn't want to leave and wasn't going to go quietly or without a fight, which caused all sorts of legal hassles.

Around the same time, my MS flared up and I was once again really poorly. I was so poorly that I knew, deep down, I'd be unable to work in the building and renovating trade any more. I was gutted as it was all I knew, other than my mediumship.

I had another, huge, life changing decision to make. It broke my heart, but I knew it was the right thing to do.

I had to give up work, and that meant giving up my business. The company I had worked so hard to grow. The company that had, inevitably, housed my family and I, fed us and nurtured us.

But I knew it was the right thing to do.

I continued to run my healing and development circles in Crawley and that helped to keep me occupied for a little while, but not working and being so ill was beginning to take its toll on my mental health and emotional wellbeing.

Once the tenant-who-didn't-want-to-leave finally did vacate, I moved in there, in Northgate. I knew it wouldn't be permanent as, by now, my now ex-wife and I we going through a bitter divorce battle. Plus, I didn't want to stay in a house that was meant to be our investment for our future, together.

Moving around and being in the property that was meant to be our pension fund, didn't help my mental health one iota. I found myself spiralling into a depression that I had never experienced before. I was creeping into darker places, mentally.

I was broken.

A New Love

The divorce was finalised in 2016 and it was time for me to move on. My MS was still bad, but I was learning to live with it better.

I moved to an apartment in Horsham and tried to throw myself back into my mediumship, as that it where I found my peace.

A few months later, I met a woman through one of the circles that I had continued to run in Crawley. She was lovely. She had three children, but it seemed the two eldest took quite a disliking to me.

The relationship still blossomed, despite the opinions of her elder two children.

It was around this time that I decided to learn more about EFT. Emotional Freedom Technique is something that had always been very interested in. EFT is used to help release negative emotions caused by physical, emotional or mental trauma and it works by tapping on acupressure meridian points on the body.

I went to Brighton and took a course on it and while I was there, I found myself discovering a new, revolutionary method called Matrix Reimprinted, which claims to help unlock long forgotten memories, including those that our subconscious has blocked out for self-preservation.

I found it totally mind blowing and decided to give it a try for myself.

It was here that all the memories of my child abuse resurfaced and I suddenly remembered why we had upped and left Wales to move to Crawley. I recalled memories that hurt me so bad, no wonder my subconscious had buried them away. I remembered telling my Dad about our neighbour and the wooden sailboat. I'm sure it was the very next day we left.

Reliving those awful memories hurt me, but now I was able to process that pain and trauma properly. I was able to evolve and learn from it.

A few months later, I remember, I took my new girlfriend away. We went up North, back to my hometown in Derbyshire for a weekend. We went to this beautiful little pub.

"If you ever propose to me, please do it here," she said.

A few months later we took another little trip up North. I had bought an engagement ring, remembering what she had said to me on our last visit.

In that same little pub, I proposed. She said yes!

But my happiness was short lived. When we returned home and her children found out, well, let's just say, they we not very happy about it. The very next day, my Fiancée called off the engagement. I was gutted. I actually couldn't believe it. I thought we were solid, despite what her elder children thought of me. She tried to give me the ring back, but I refused to accept it. I wanted her to keep it.

A Love Revisited

I had called upon a friend who lived in Newdigate and asked if I could stay. As it happened, her cabin was unoccupied and she offered it to me to stay in it for as long as I needed.

I was so very grateful.

At the beginning of 2018, I visited Dubai and Bahrain to work doing my mediumship.

When I arrived back to the UK, my ex-fiancée came to pick me up from the airport and give me a lift back home. She asked if we could meet up later that evening for dinner. I agreed.

We met in Horsham for a meal, and I noticed that she was wearing the engagement ring that I had proposed to her with.

She said she was sorry, that she had made a mistake and that she loved me. She wanted us to try again. To be honest with you, it was all very romantic. My feelings for her had not dissolved. I did still love her too.

So, we tried again. We moved in together and things were great.

However, within a few months, we found ourselves bickering and rowing over the most silliest things. I could see the distance growing between us.

Towards the end of the year, my Fiancée's sister and daughter were involved in a horrific car accident, which, sadly, resulted in the death of my Fiancée's niece. It was so tragic.

We went to Northern Ireland for the funeral, which was attended by many family members and friends. One person who was part of the congregation was my Fiancée's ex-boyfriend from almost twenty years before. They began chatting, flirting even, and I could feel the energy between them growing stronger and stronger and I knew, deep down, it was over between us.

Sure enough, as soon as we were back home, she called it off with me again.

I wasn't going back this time. We were over and there was no going back. But, my heart was broken.

For the next year or so, I threw myself more and more into my mediumship, helping spirits get their messages to loved ones here. To give message of hope and love.

That helped me heal my broken heart.

Following My Dream

I flew back to the United States in December of 2019. I spent Christmas in Las Vegas, taking in the sights. The place is incredible! All the casinos and the amazing water fountain outside the Bellagio.

Then, I drove down to California to see the new year in with some friends. I had a great time. However, once again, I found myself thinking about what it would be like to work, even live there in the USA.

I came back to England with a new dream. I wanted to go and live and work where I felt most welcome.

Then Covid hit and all my plans and dreams fell by the wayside as the world seemed to stop. A pandemic of epic proportions, not seen by anyone living today. Lots of people died. Some people struggled to get basic amenities and food. Communities pulled together to help the elderly and vulnerable to get medicines and shopping. Our health service was overwhelmed with sick people, struggling to breathe due to the effects of Covid.

It was a difficult time for almost the whole population of the entire planet.

Once the world began to open up again, I realised that it was time to put my plans into action.

My Encounters And Experiences

Readings

Shaun's Story

It was about 3 months after losing our son Connor, whose life was taken by an act of brutal violence, that I said to my Wife that, if there was an afterlife, then we should go looking for our son. My Niece, who lives in Horley, had told me that there was a good spiritualist church in nearby Three Bridges. I then searched online to find that a medium by the name of Nigel Gaff was there that evening, so off we went.

Nigel gave some really good messages to people in the audience. We longed for a message, and just when it seemed it wasn't going to be, we heard "can the lady in the white blouse stand up". We were overjoyed. I stood with my wife, at this time both shaking. Straight away he said of a pain in the back of his head, and went on to say I have your son with me! Elation for us and we were blown away with the things that he told us, things he couldn't have known unless he was a family member. We were buzzing.

After the evening finished, I made my way to the stage to thank him. He gave me a card and said to call. I rang the next day and agreed to have a private reading with him. Again, he gave us more.

Since then, we know that our beloved Son is safe, ok and loves us dearly. I gave Nigel my number and said that I would contact him in the future. Nigel's gift is heaven sent. This was proven beyond all doubt eight months later. I hadn't heard from him and vice versa, but I came home this particular day to find my Wife laying on the kitchen floor, in which I can only describe as a state of hysteria, sobbing. She felt like she couldn't go on any more. Whilst lifting her off the floor, my phone bleeped.

Obviously I ignored it for some minutes until I had calmed my Wife down. Once she had composed herself and walked out of the room, I checked my phone. It was a text from Nigel Gaff. It read...

"Tell Connor's Mum he loves her, and he really is ok."

I couldn't believe that the message had come at this time! We were elated. I truly believe that at that moment, we began to heal.

Nigel has a wonderful gift, and has helped us survive the nightmare we were living.

Connor is fine and doing wonderful things on the other side. For Nigel we are truly grateful. .

Sue's Story

My Sister, Mum and I went for a reading with Nigel. We all went together as we were hoping to hear from my Dad.

But it was my Granddad who was the main person to come through. Nigel told us how my Granddad died, how old he was and that he drove lorries for a living and lived in London - all true.

Nigel then spoke of seeing my granddad playing cards and talking about "The Great Train Robbery", which was amazing, because it was my Granddad's friend who arranged all the cars for the job.

It's lovely to know our family are still all around us.

Nicki's Story

I first saw Nigel Gaff at Three Bridges Spiritualist Church. He'd been recommended by a friend, so I went a few weeks after my mum had passed with cancer.

Nigel did not know me, or anything about me, yet he brought through two members of my family; my Mum and my Uncle.

Uncannily, he also called me by my nickname, which would not make sense to anyone except me. I remember Nigel looking at me quizzically and asking what it meant and I clarified that it was a nickname.

You could hear the gasps in the audience! He correctly described my Mum and the way she passed and gave me a very comforting message using language that my Mum used.

Emma Lane's Story *I was asked literally thirty minutes before the Connor Saunders evening if I would like to attend with a friend. I had given up hope of 'Dad' coming through to me after a previous reading with a different medium left me heartbroken. I had patiently waited for 18 years.*

My feelings were, I don't know the medium; my name isn't on a list anywhere; what have I got to lose? Although, looking back, I was desperate, as I even took a picture of Dad along.

The readings were coming thick and fast, which was pleasing for many. I was just about to relax and put my picture away in my bag when I heard Nigel say - I have man who is asking me to sing an Elvis song!! My heart jumped. My Dad had been an Elvis impersonator. Trying to keep calm and cool I didn't want to give any signs, then Nigel pointed in my direction. He said that he had a Dad/Granddad, who liked a cigarette and even named the brand!

He told me that Dad had passed and it was the right time for him and he was tired and is at peace. This is the main comfort as my Dad died suddenly and very young. Nigel then said that it would have been his birthday and he thanked me for recognising it would have been. Now, I didn't grow up in Sussex so not even my friends would have known my Dad. I feel at peace and can finally let Dad go.

Thank you Nigel.

Anon

I had a reading with Nigel and one of the messages I received was quite amazing and out of the blue as it had no connection to my family. Nigel asked if I had known anyone that had served in the army and had passed in Afghanistan, which I had not. Nigel was insistent that this gentleman wanted to pass on a message to me which, again, I disputed. Nigel explained that he saw the gentleman in an army 'desert' uniform and had passed suddenly, being blown up by a car bomb.

Nigel had images of seeing a plane land in the UK, unloading an army casket and approximated this was 18 months to 2 years previous. It then occurred to me that some time ago, I was out with friends and was introduced to a woman. After talking to her for some time she told me her fiancé had died in Afghanistan and it was the 2nd anniversary of his death. Nigel explained the gentleman wanted to thank me for spending time with his girlfriend. This was an unexpected message; one that was heartfelt and a privilege to receive.

It's Genuine, Believe Me!

I particularly remember another message when I was at a house party. I was with a friend of mine who is a psychic artist and we used to work together quite a lot. I would give the mediumship and she would draw those who came through. I can't draw to save my life, if I did they would all end up looking like *Shrek*, so I did the clairvoyant side of the mediumship.

I remember there were quite a few people at this party.

We had a break and a cup of tea. During the break, this young guy came over to me. He was from Scotland, very polite and pleasant but then asked something that kind of shocked me.

"Do you use plants?"

"What do you mean by that?" I asked.

Well, I knew what he meant - I just couldn't believe he came over and asked it.

"No, I don't," I replied firmly. It gave me the hump to be honest. If I had to resort to that, it would be the end, I wouldn't do it anymore.

He then asked me: "The lady who was sitting at the front, whose grandmother came through, do you know her?"

"No," I said, "I've never seen her before."

I know you might find it hard to believe. He was an airline pilot, clearly a clever man but he didn't believe a word of it. Anyway, the evening went on and more and more messages came out for everybody. Eventually he was the only one left who hadn't had a message, so I reluctantly came to him and I remember saying:

"I don't know what I'm going to get with you but I'll see what happens." Truth be told, I didn't really want to speak to him after his comments earlier in the evening.

But I linked in and a gentleman made himself aware to me and that, when he was alive, he had taught this young man to drive. As I told him this, the pilot burst into tears. Then the evidence got stronger. This gentleman was a very dear friend of this young pilot and was very close to him.

When the evening had finished, the young pilot came over to me and shook my hand.

"I would never have believed in any of this," he said, "but what you've just shared with me has blown me away." He went home to Scotland, and saw the family who had lost the gentleman that had passed and gave evidence of his ongoing survival.

I was talking to one young lady, at a different meeting, when I knew there was a young man connected with her who had gone out of life very suddenly. One minute he was there and the next he was gone, through a motor bike accident. All their plans for the future were instantaneously undone. They were planning a house move and he also had a house in Spain. The young lady confirmed all this and I looked to her mother who also confirmed that he had been very much a part of their family.

And then, as I was working, I was suddenly aware of this great big noisy tractor coming in. I could sense it was this young lady's Uncle and her Mother confirmed that yes, it was. He had died when she was in her late twenties, so her daughter was just a little schoolgirl.

He was a very jokey sort of person, who was lots of fun; he liked practical jokes; loved Christmas and worked very hard. The Mother, Gabrielle, confirmed he was a farmer.

Well, he came riding in on this chugging tractor and then she sadly had to acknowledge that, yes, he did work on a tractor and that this is what killed him. He'd ended up in a river with the tractor on top of him.

Gabrielle: *Nigel was describing my brother, Michael, and how he died on his tractor and he was this jokey person who was lots of fun. It's interesting that my son has a bit of a water phobia, and he used to have dreams about water and being trapped and not able to get out! In a passport photo he showed me one day, with his hair all brushed back; he looked just like my brother, Michael, for a minute.*

A Glimpse Into The Spirit World

Gaye Smart, who had done an interview with me for her book, came to see me. I knew her husband had died not too long ago, but she made it clear she was hoping that somebody else would come through.

Suddenly, I had this explosive pain in my head; a terrible headache and I could sense it was a woman who was dying from this.

Gaye: *I was disappointed at first, since it was my Mother I was hoping for and she had died from bronchial pneumonia, so that I had been expecting breathing problems. But then I suddenly remembered that, since she'd died suddenly in Ibiza, 42 years ago, and the doctor couldn't speak English, he drew a little drawing for me to explain what killed her. What he drew was a cerebral haemorrhage, which shot up to her head and exploded!*

Then I felt suffocated and I couldn't get my breath. The surge of emotions overpowered me.

I could see her mother so clearly after that and she was showing herself with this fox fur around her neck. She was wearing lace with a smart hat with her hair done beautifully, looking elegant and glamorous.

Now, she began to show me castles, valleys and a whole make-believe world of rivers, flowers and light which she said were all in the spirit realm. She described how they were all real to her as she has created them in spirit. She is now free and no longer restricted in life. She told how myth and magic are reality in the spiritual realm. She said it's like Harry Potter land.

She explained how wonder comes out of spiritual energy, to give to those who can write or paint inspiration to recreate that wonder; for in spirit you can reconstruct there from the best of what you had here. She told how you can relive it since, in spirit, you create your own dimensions. She was giving me a view of the imaginable worlds, just like the World of Terry Pratchett.

The mother came in really close and sometimes this makes me dizzy when they get too close. She mentioned June, and Gaye said that she had died in June. She confirmed to me the truth of how we continue after this life as this life is a kind of illusion. I then had to say that, what I always feel is that life is just a book someone has written, but this is a book by the greatest author going!

I could then see something about Gaye's sister, who is still alive, and I told Gaye about her and about how they are so different from each other, with a completely different focus in life, which she confirmed.

Next I could see something about a special set of pearls which their mother had loved so much and wanted to be passed on to her only granddaughter.

Then Gaye's father came through in his army uniform from his younger years and he was saying how much he had loved being in the army. He described the tanks and that he had been in the tank regiment. But then this man started saying to me that he didn't believe in any of this stuff about spirit. He was talking to me from the spiritual realm, saying he had grown up in a family where he wasn't allowed to believe in any of it and that this brought such a conflict for him. He was so adamant and his emotions were so powerful that, for a split second, I questioned myself as to whether I really was talking to him in spirit!

Next to come through was Gaye's Grandfather in his plus fours, playing golf as he loved to do and he was a glamorous man, clever and a deep thinker.

Gaye: *I was astounded when I was talking to my Daughter, later on (she is the only granddaughter to my Mother) to find out something that I never knew which was that some five years ago my Sister, in New Zealand, had indeed passed on a set of pearls to my daughter which came from my Mother. There was a note attached saying: 'These are from your Grandmother as she would have wanted you to have them.'*

Nigel, on that afternoon, not only gave my Mother back to me but also brought her through in the role of grandmother which was a role she never managed to fulfil while she was alive.

156

Spirits in the Ramada

I remember a job I once done at the Ramada Hotel at Heathrow, down the Bath Road. It's been re-built now (good job as it was falling to bits at the time). It was a really tired property and run down but I guess that's my business; refurbishment - the more run down, the better for me.

I was working with my friend, Danny, who is very spiritual and would have made a fantastic medium, although he never worked with his gifts. I remember we were talking about spiritual matters and, as we did so, the doors on this landing kept slamming shut on their own

I knew something was going on. By the end of the day there was an energy following Danny about, and she took a fancy to him. This lady had got herself trapped in the hotel. Haven't got a clue why, but she was there nevertheless. She got in the van with us when we went home, nice and cosy.

For some reason she found Danny quite interesting.

He's a sensitive man and gentle too, (don't tell him I told you so). She was with him most of the way home and I managed to dislodge her and then she wanted to stay with me; story of my life - strange women following me about. I didn't mind. I think it was my fault any way where I had kept chattering on about spiritualism and she was obviously listening to us, so stay with me she did! She stayed all night actually. She didn't stop talking, went on and on and drove me round the twist until eventually I went round to Danny's house.

"Look mate," I said, "I've still got this bird with me. She won't leave me alone."

But, together, we were able to send her back to the light.

This was the strangest thing because Danny and I could see her going. She didn't want to, mind, it was a bit of a struggle, but we got there in the end. She had a tear in her eye as she was going bless her; she was scared she just didn't know what was going to happen to her. We watched as she went into the light. She'd been trapped on the earth plane for quite a while. Then she found us, knew we could help her and we did, free at last.

The whole feeling of her leaving me made me feel very sick; sick to my stomach as she went home. There were many occasions like that where I've released a spirit from this earth plane, back home. This is where we all go to and where we're all from; we all go back to the light. This is what we do for our soul to grow and gain experience of whatever we are here to learn, that's what it's all about.

Trapped Spirit

Coincidentally, Danny and I were working again at a woman's house in West Sussex. I don't believe in coincidence and nor does any medium because coincidence doesn't exactly happen, it isn't a real thing. It is all co-orchestrated so that we live it here, and we put it down to coincidence but the majority of our experiences here are pre-destined.

Anyway, we went to decorate this lady's bedroom. There was something about her that I really liked. She looked at me and smiled and she could see something in me as I could see something in her. She took us into her bedroom and left us there because she wanted the wallpaper stripped and the room redecorated. There was the strangest feeling in this room. It was a warm day but it was ice cold in her bedroom and there was a pulsating energy over the bed.

I immediately knew there was a spirit there and it turned out it was the lady's son who had tragically died in a motorbike accident. Her grief was so strong she couldn't let her son go back to the light. Her love for him was so intense that it held him within this earth environment; he was stuck in her bedroom. He couldn't go home. We clearly weren't there just to decorate; I believed this was a ruse.

Ultimately our job was to set this young man free.

You don't actually have to be in the presence of a spirit to help them travel on. He wanted to go home, so it wasn't as if I had to try and force him away.

He really wanted to go back to the light. He was fed up with being trapped in his mother's bedroom and it was time for him to move on. He knew there was more, I think he had seen the light but wasn't able to leave his mum.

So we left the room and went and sat in my van and I concentrated and focused until I was able, through my thoughts, to open the door for him to the spirit realms.

Then he was able to step through and he went home. When we went back to the room, the temperature had completely changed, he was no longer there.

The whole energy had gone and it was just so calm in the room, whereas before, it had been electric. Anyway, we stripped the wallpaper off the room and, as we stripped it, we found a picture that had been drawn on the walls which had been scraped into the plaster.

This picture was like a child's drawing, a picture of a house with windows and a door just as a child would have drawn, with a chimney pot. Above the chimney and going up to what would have been the sky was a line. This straight line was going away from the chimney and as it was going further up there was a line crossing it, stopping it. It was connected with this young man who had been trapped in this bedroom for a good few years and wanted to go home.

He had learned what his energy was and what it could do and somehow he could draw under the wallpaper. It was the spookiest thing I'd ever seen and Danny and I both knew it was showing us that he was trapped in this room. Nobody had picked it up and it wasn't by accident that we were there, not at all.

Do you know, a year later I questioned what I had experienced as I couldn't quite believe what had happened. I was walking around my local town and who would I bump into on the very day but his mother just when I was thinking and questioning: 'What happened there?'

She spoke to me and had a chat and then I knew it wasn't my imagination, it was real. I've had a few instances where I've helped spirit on their way back to the spirit realms.

I've seen glimpses, as well, of the afterlife but they don't let us get too close. We are only allowed to see so much for good reason.

We only get to see that reality when we go home because, if you could see the beauty, the wonder, the love and the comfort and warmth of the spirit realms, you wouldn't want to be here anymore. So it is a good job we can't see it, and it's a good job we can't get there.

You know, life is for the living and we need to make the most of this life or try our very best to do so, because this is the living time. Even if you are depressed and fed up, it is important to see your time here out, since we're not here for long. Even though it may be very hard at times, you will be glad you saw it through when you get home; and you will get home; you will eventually see the truth and you'll be amazed.

An Unexpected Call

In the early 2010's, a girl of about seventeen or eighteen years old came to see me, mainly for a bit of coaching, as opposed to a reading.

Strangely enough, though, I'd picked up that there was some kind of situation with her and her father; that there'd been a row and they were estranged.

We got talking.

"Don't be surprised if your father contacts you at some point," I said.

"No, I don't think that's going to happen," she replied.

Anyway, I'd asked her to switch her mobile phone off, which she did, and she placed it next to her on the table. I was talking and telling her about her father and repeated: "Don't be surprised if he contacts you."

She dismissed that again. As I worked with her, she suddenly announced that her phone had just turned itself on. She was really shocked.

"My God," she said, "my phone's just turned itself on."

I continued talking to her and, some ten minutes later, her phone rang.

"I don't believe it," she announced. Yes, you guessed, it was her father and she hadn't spoken to him for two years.

Well that goes to show you what spiritual energies can do. Her phone was off, as I ask everybody I see to turn their phones off when I am working with them. Then it turned itself on!

I knew her father would be in contact with her - I just didn't think it would be that quick! Spirit really are amazing.

That was just one instance that was a bit strange.

Spooky Manor

I remember a time, quite a few years ago, when I had to go up north with a colleague where we were installing alarms on computers. Back then I was working as a medium.

One day, I was intuitively drawn to a guest house. It was a really old manor which was originally owned by a shipping tycoon back in the sixteenth or seventeenth century. Then he sold the property and it was taken over by a nunnery.

I'd better not tell you what it was called but, the lady that ran it was so very nice, and these are only my experiences, so I can't speak for anybody else.

It was comfortable, clean and well-furnished, so no moans there. This nunnery and these nuns, and it's a bit of a spooky tale, well, it all turned bad. They got into all sorts of particularly unpleasant stuff. Satanism in fact.

I stayed there overnight with a colleague, Kevin, and, my God, the amount of happenings - talk about bumps in the night! All night long there were doors slamming, floorboards were creaking, and stuff was moving around and the amount of spiritual activity within that house was tremendous. And there were particularly unpleasant energies in the house as well.

I remember very clearly that we stayed there for a week and then we ended up going to stay in a Travel Inn because it became not a nice place to be; well certainly not for a medium, as I was aware of the energies. I am sure for the majority of people it was fine.

It was probably going back maybe thirty years ago now, but it was an experience for me; something to help me grow and learn with. So that was quite a good one. In fact I remember how I was running a healing circle at the time and one of my healers picked up that there was a lot of unpleasantness around me within my aura; an energy that related back to that house. It was fine, though, we did some healing and I was back to normal - whatever normal is.

The Missing Tooth

I also did a reading for a lady who had seen me work in the Spiritualist Church and liked my humour and the way I worked with spirit. I can only work the way I do.

Do you know, I have tried to work like other mediums? I just can't do it, I can only be who I am.

Anyway, this lady came to see me and she brought her daughter with her. I didn't know the daughter was coming.

"Oh, I've seen you in church," said the mother, "and I finally plucked up courage to come and see you because I am quite scared."

They sat down in my study and a lady came through who had passed to spirit with breathing difficulties and the lady said, "oh, it was my Nan." It was the daughter's great grandmother.

"She passed with difficulty," I said, "and she had stomach cancer as well."

"Yes, she did," the mother said as she nodded in agreement.

I described lots of things about the woman who had passed, and it was all one hundred percent right.

"You know, I've been going to a Spiritualist Church for two years hoping to hear from my Nan," said the mother, "and she's never, ever come through. I've never had a message from her."

"Funnily enough," I said, "the spirit chooses the medium. It's not the other way around."

We don't choose who comes through, no medium can. Who comes through, comes through. All a medium can do is to open a door, they can't demand that someone specific comes through. But they can always ask.

This lady's grandmother came through and I don't know whether she was waiting for me or if she found it was more easy to communicate with me. I must admit, I don't know how it all works, but they have their own way of working and I just have to go along with it.

As the reading continued, her grandmother came through and she spoke about her tooth.

"Why is your Grandmother pointing to one particular tooth?" I asked. "The one in the upper front which is missing? She's quite annoyed about this."

"Oh my God," she replied. "When she went in for surgery, she had to have a scope down into her tummy. She had stomach cancer and they pushed this scope down and knocked her front tooth out." Her grandmother was really quite concerned about her tooth that had gone missing. She was annoyed about it and that they'd done this.

To return to this woman with her daughter, I then mentioned about the woman's partner.

"Your partner doesn't believe in any of this?" I asked, but I said it as more of a statement. "He thinks everything about spirit and spiritual matters is a load of rubbish." Now, as I think I have mentioned before, spirits like it when we are happy and funny and high vibrational energy. And often, they too are humorous when they connect with me.

"That's right," she replied. "He doesn't believe in any of it, he thinks it's complete hogwash!"

"So, who was the gentleman who worked in the kitchen?" I asked.

This was his real father and he was in the navy. He came through and so did his stepfather, and most of his uncles. And she said she would tell him when she went home. She did say it would be difficult for him to accept and I can understand this. I do know that people struggle with the concept about how dead people can come back to talk with us and communicate with us but they do.

As I have previously explained, I am clairsentient, which means that I can feel the energy of the spirit which has passed by feeling *how* they passed. This means that if they had lung cancer or if they had a heart attack or a brain tumour, I can feel what it was that took them back to the spirit realms.

It can be quite a strong feeling, although at other times it is not.

Going Back To The Light

I would like to recount a memory of my friend, Peter, who is one of the most incredible mediums that I have ever known and he has led a very interesting life, in fact, the most interesting life of anyone I have ever met.

 He went diamond mining in Sierra Leone and was taken to hospital because he was very ill. He actually died in hospital and found himself back in the spiritual realm, in a huge crimson room so big you couldn't see from one end to the other.

He said the feeling was that of being in the most lovely warm cosy blanket ever and he heard a voice say to him, "well, Peter, you have a choice, you can go back or you can come and stay with us. It's up to you."

He said the next thing he knew was that he found himself waking up in the hospital.

He decided he didn't want to go back home, to the spiritual realm, as he knew he still had work left to do here. But he later said, "next time my bags will be packed." And he's waiting to go because he won't make that mistake again!

There have been many books written about what it's like to be in the light and I've had my own experiences. I've seen into it myself. I've seen the most beautiful oceans, the most wonderful mountain ranges and the most incredible places you can imagine - spirit realms are vast, limitless. Everything is energy and we're all just energy. We explore and experience that energy when we go back home and we make our reality there.

Of course there is nothing in the spirit realms that is anything like we have here because it's not a physical realm, it's metaphysical, where all is energy. The true reality of your being and your true home is there and it certainly isn't here.

I'm OK!

I did a big demonstration with a friend of mine, some years ago, and there were about two hundred and fifty people in the auditorium. We had radio microphones, and as I started to work and establish my links, it was then my turn to speak.

As I looked round, there was a young man sitting in the centre aisle. He was a tall guy.

"I want to come to you, sir," I said as I headed over towards him.

I was drawn to him. Spirit were guiding me to him for a reason and when I started working with him it all became clear why I was drawn to him.

"You are planning to go to Australia?' I asked, but it was rather more of a factual statement than a rhetorical question.

"Yes, I am," he replied.

"Well, you've got a friend here who died in a motor accident. He wants me to tell you that he's okay."

Then a tear appeared in the corner of his eye and he said his best friend had died in a motor accident three or four months before this demonstration. In the car that evening, he had said out loud: 'If you are really still around, if you still exist, I want you to come through tonight and I want you to let me know you're OK.'

And the message as it came through was just that. He was okay. This was exactly as he'd asked for when he was in the car driving to the demonstration.

The evidence then rolled on.

During the demonstrations, I was also able to tell the young man all sorts of stuff about his life and what he was going to do in the future.

"Your friend is going to be with you all the way," I said, and I got the feeling that they had a very close bond when his friend was here, almost like they were brothers. They were so close, they loved each other dearly as good friends do. That was a lovely message I've never forgotten - an interesting one really.

The Missing Tickets

I also remember one that was quite amusing.

I did a demonstration with a colleague at a house party where there were eight or ten people. I came to the lady whose house it was.

"I'm told that you've lost something that you were looking for in the house," I said, "and you can't find it anywhere."

"Yes, that's right. I have," she said.

"Your Granddad is saying that he's hidden it and doesn't want you to have it."

She smiled and came to me afterwards and explained to me that she had lost something and she couldn't find it. They were tickets to see a celebrity that her Granddad didn't particularly like. I won't name names, but she knew exactly what her Granddad meant and she knew he didn't like this man. He didn't want her to go, so he hid the tickets from her, and she couldn't find them.

It was bizarre. Proof again, as I couldn't have known that. Clearly, I had a link with her Grandfather and he was telling me that he wasn't going to let her find them because he didn't want her to waste her time. It was quite amusing really.

A Letter Of Love

I remember doing a party booking some years ago when I was invited round a lady's house. There were six or seven people there and I was giving messages from the spiritual realms.

Now, I remember coming to this young lady and telling her she had lost a child. She said she had.

"You still had a funeral," I said, "although this was just a baby."

"Yes, I did," she replied.

"I'm being shown that you wrote a letter and in that letter you poured out your heart, all your love and all your emotions and then you took the letter into the garden and you buried it."

This was when she burst into tears.

"Nobody knew about that. I did exactly that after the funeral and no one knew about it, I told no one. It was just me and my child. I'd lost my baby and no one knew about this letter."

It was astounding to me that Spirit was able to give me this information, which I could give to this lady, who was still clearly suffering from the loss of her child.

Over the years, I must have given thousands of messages and probably forgotten ninety nine percent of them, but these are just a few which still stick in my memory.

Clairvoyance

One of my clairvoyant experiences, where I saw the future, concerned a friend of mine who shall remain nameless for this book. He's a good friend and I used to train with him in a gym years ago. He came to see me one day when I had an office at a hotel locally where I used to work. He popped in for a coffee.

"I've met this new girl," he said. As he said that, I could see images in my mind of him settling down with her.

"You know, you're going to settle down with her, buy a detached house and have a son," I said. I could see it all laid out in front of him. Spirit had shown me the birth of his son and the house he would buy and sure enough, six months later, he settled down with her; they bought a detached house, she became pregnant and they had a little boy; exactly as I'd described.

Then, a couple of years later, he came round to see me for a chat.

"Oh," I said, "your partner's pregnant again and it's going to be a little girl."

Sure enough she was pregnant and they had a little girl.

Sometimes I can see very clearly, clairvoyantly, ahead of me because, you know, spirit sees your tomorrows today. But that's not always the case. I think it all depends on if the person in front of me is more open to it.

A friend of mine had a motorbike and I said: "You've got to get rid of that motorbike." I could see it wouldn't be good for him. He ignored my advice and that weekend he crashed. Fortunately, he was okay and didn't get injured. But then he took my advice and sold the motorbike because I just knew it was not good for him to keep it any longer.

I've done many sessions of platform mediumship over the years, where I've come to people and I remember I came to a lady and asked her what the problem with her son was.

"I've had nothing to do with my son," she said. "I haven't talked to him for the last three years."

"Well, I can see your son getting married."

"Yes, he is getting married," she replied.

"And you will be invited to the wedding," I said.

"No, I'm sorry you're wrong that won't happen," she said as she shook her head.

Six months later, I was back at the same church working and that same lady was there. She hurried up to see me and she was carrying a photo album.

"These are the pictures of my son's wedding,' she told me. "And you were one hundred percent correct. A couple of days after you'd given me that reading, I had a phone call from my son inviting me to his wedding in America."

This has happened consistently for me over many years, certainly when I do evenings of mediumship. At a demonstration, I can often see what's going to happen. It isn't me, of course, you must understand, none of these are my abilities. All I am is a channel for spirit to work through and that's what they do.

They just work through me and give me the information to pass on to people. It is all done on a love vibration. It's because they love us so much, they come through with encouragement and with love and support for us; that's what a medium's job is. A medium always aims to give hope, light and to raise peoples' vibrations.

I have heard instances of mediums giving bad messages but that's not how it should be. If a medium sees something unpleasant, then they have no right to share that with someone. Mediums carry a lot of responsibility and if they're not trained sufficiently, nor wise enough, they can ruin peoples' lives by a misplaced word because people listen to mediums so much. I've heard so many times about how people come in and put their lives into what a medium has told them.

I've had people coming to me saying, "I saw a medium who said I wasn't going to make old bones and that I am going to die young."

That's just so unethical, they shouldn't be working and giving out such negative messages.

Messages should always bring hope and contain love and happiness and should never be any kind of message of sadness or despondency. There are too many people who are quite happy to give that information and I think it is not right. I feel this is wrong because it can ruin peoples' lives and then they sit and they wait for these bad things to happen. Then, unfortunately, because they're so worried, they're thinking all these negative thoughts all the time, they manifest it themselves through The Law of Attraction; they make it happen for themselves because of their fear, and it's an awful thing. I'm sorry but I really don't agree with this way of working.

I work with a very strong ethical code and all the mediums I know also work with this code. If you have nothing good to say to someone, if you have no positive message to give, then you shouldn't be giving a message to them at all.

Messages should be positive and loving and the truth.

Angels

I want to talk a bit about angels and my experience with of them.

I'm a Reiki Master, as well as a medium, and I trained in Reiki healing. Reiki is about channelling healing energy. Most mediums and clairvoyants start off on a healing road. They want to help people; the love from spirit comes through the healer and I'm no different.

Over the years I have trained and attuned my own students. Attunement is tuning the student in to the healing energy.

Anyway, there was this time that I was doing a Reiki attunement session quite a few years ago, at a friend's house. There were three people there all sat in a line and I was attuning the first student. You basically carry this out by placing symbols in the chakras - unlocking them to the healing energy.

I'll never forget, I turned round and sitting in the corner of the room was an angel. I swear to God this angel was bent over double because it was so big. I could see the angel looking at me and smiling and it was just beautiful, absolutely beautiful. I froze on the spot and stared for what felt like ages, though it was probably only seconds, but I stood there admiring this beautiful thing and thinking "My God, I can't believe I'm actually looking at an angel."

I carried on with the Reiki class; the student must have thought I had gone off for a walk or something as I'd spent time admiring the angel. By the end of the attunement, it had gone.

My other experience was quite a few years ago now in Essex when I did a demonstration with a fellow medium. We were at a lady's home and she had cleared out all the furniture in her lounge and turned it into a spiritual meeting room just for this demonstration. During the session, I kept being drawn to a gentleman standing at the back of the room and I felt very uneasy with his energy. He kept staring at me and I didn't feel very good, in fact I was quite intimidated by him.

As I finished my work, everyone was getting up and walking out but I was frozen to the spot. I remember a feeling of heat around my entire body and, as this feeling came over me, I could feel feathers. I knew there was angel energy around me. The feathers closed around me, around my chest, stomach and my head and it was as if they were putting all this protection all over me. Then all my feelings of anxiety and nervousness from this particular individual left me immediately and I walked forward with this energy around me for the rest of the night.

It took everything that was dark in the world away from me immediately and it felt wonderful.

Then there was another occasion when I was picking up a colleague of mine, Peter Richards, as we were doing an evening of mediumship together. He lives opposite a multiple sclerosis hospital which is a respite centre for people with severe MS (multiple sclerosis).

Along the front of the building there is a picket fence which is about four or five foot high. It was a winter's evening, dark and cold and, as I sat in my car, something caught my eye.

There was a flash of light at the right hand corner of my vision and, sitting on this fence, there must have been about four or five angels and they were talking to each other. I looked across and one of them saw me and they could see that I could see them. As my mouth dropped open they smiled. I looked on in amazement, then I looked away and turned the radio on thinking it was all my imagination and the song "Angels" by Robbie Williams started playing. I thought how about that for a coincidence. As you know, I don't believe in coincidence, I guess it was that bit of evidence I needed.

I have grown to become reasonably interested in angels. I have realised that angels are real; they are the foot soldiers of God and they have carte blanche in this world. They work with the God energy and they are right up there in terms of their authority. They can do what they see fit; they can do what they are here to do. Your ascended soul, over many lifetimes, reaches the God figure, and as your soul joins with the God energy, you have the opportunity to be one with the angelic realms, to be part of God's creative force. Basically, to help just like God does. That is what Heaven is, the ultimate goal of your soul.

You ascend and ascend and keep growing. That is why you have multiple lives. The only reason we are all here is to have an experience.

This is nothing more than a big university, a big school and it is a very well-orchestrated and sophisticated illusion. There are no such things as coincidences. Everything happens for a reason. It's a bit like 'The Matrix' in that everything you see around you is like a veil of secrecy, and you're only seeing what you're allowed to see.

Evil Spirits

As a medium, one of the questions I often get asked, and it's a common one for some reason, is about evil spirits; the spirits who aren't particularly pleasant.

Well, if you weren't very nice when you were here in this world; if you were an evil person when you were here, then all the time your spirit is attached to this realm you're going to be evil as well. Yes there are evil spirits but they're only a reflection of the life they led in this world.

But remember, it is not the dead that will hurt you, it is only the living.

The reality is that sometimes it is difficult for evil spirits, or people who have done bad things, to go home because when you pass, no one judges you, you know the God figure doesn't judge you; you judge yourself and that's how it works. If you've done bad things here, then you judge yourself and often you don't allow yourself to go home because you feel too scared and guilty. You feel you can't go home, you will be as you were when you lived here.

When your energy leaves your body, when you die, that energy is freed into this dimension to enable you to 'pass over' to the spiritual one. But, if you don't go over, for whatever reason (through guilt of what you've done, for example), then you stay trapped here in this dimension. Although you might feel free when you pass, you're still trapped in this world and then you will be what you were when you lived. We call these earth plane spirits.

It's not until you go home and transcend this existence that you are then what you are meant to be, which is a spirit energy. When you get home, you're totally free.

Then you will judge yourself.

Karma is real and you'll make the decision to pay back that which you have done. You'll make the decision because karma has its place. It is the part of your soul which was here on this earth plane, which has to be in balance when it returns home.

Often the only way to balance it is to have a life. And, to have a life is to experience that which you did that was wrong. If you've wronged someone in a certain way or you've wronged a group of people, whatever you might have done, then you will have to pay that back.

The universe has to have a balance.

Karma is a real thing; it is a reality; that is true. There is always a constant and that constant has to be in balance.

If you have done good things here, in this life, then that is the balance and if you have done bad or wrong things in this life then you'll have to balance that as well. It is the same old, same old, an eye for an eye and a tooth for a tooth; balance will always be had.

But it is not consciously your decision.

It never is.

Although we think we're in control consciously, it is inevitably our soul's decision and that's what makes the decisions for you. It's your soul and nothing else. Karma is a real thing and balance of the karmic field will be had. The scales must always be in balance. It has to work out, it always will and it always has and that's never going to change.

Suicide

One of the things I'm often asked is about people who take their own lives, people who commit suicide.

I've brought through many who have but I'm uncomfortable with that because often, when someone has committed suicide, they were in a very dark place in their lives and they bring that energy back with them. I also find it hard because I feel their immense sorrow and sadness, for them and their loved ones still here.

The message is always the same. A big 'sorry' for all the pain that they caused but, as with all spirit, they are fine and are 'home'.

You know, they go to the realms of spirit, they go home, like we all do.

No one judges them there, they simply judge themselves.

They're back there in spirit with the love when they go home so they're not cast into darkness as some medium once said to me (who should never have been working as a medium, but that's another story). They go home just like anybody else does. You know, when somebody takes their own life, I understand, I really do, because people get to that desperately dark place in their lives. They are at their wits end and they just don't know where to turn.

"Suicide is just the coward's way out!" someone said to me once. I'm sorry but I don't agree with that. Actually it takes a lot of guts and a lot of bravery to terminate your own life here because the conscious natural instinct is for survival and human beings would do anything to survive. It's most definitely not the coward's way out, so I've never agreed with that statement.

But when you go home, when we all go home, it's like a light bulb moment. Suddenly you realise 'Hey, I'm back home and my entire life, as wonderful as it was, with the good and the bad points, was simply just a kind of illusion.' The world and all the other universes and the galaxies that God has constructed are all based on this type of illusion. Your real home, where you truly exist, where you exist permanently and where you can never die, is in the realms of spirit.

In the dimension of spirit, there is no death. There is no pain, hunger, tiredness, depression, anger, selfishness or jealousy. There is nothing we have here in that existence.

What lies there is beauty and love beyond all measure, which we could never understand here. So when you eventually go back home from this world and the light comes on, it's, 'wow, I understand now. I know what it's all been about. I understand what my life was. Now I know why I had my life, I know why I met this person, had this child and married this individual.' Your life is mapped out before you come.

But, of course, we all have free will, of that there is no doubt. As much as we have free will, there is also a grander plan which spirit has for us to live our lives, to help us grow, to achieve and to manifest into something more beautiful when we go home.

Quite often, people tell me how they're scared to die.

"Never be scared to die," I will tell them in return.

In some cultures it is celebrated. Death here means existence elsewhere, in another realm. The spiritual realm.

When people go home, there is rejoicing and parties because they have a deeper spiritual knowledge and they know that when they go home they return to beauty, love, kindness and happiness.

Celebrities And The Famous

Now I must tell you about some of the spiritual work I've done with celebrities. Well, I haven't *done it* with celebrities as, when you go back to spirit, whether you're rich or famous, King or Queen, or whoever you are, you're the same as everybody else.

Queen Victoria
In 2012 or thereabouts, I visited Osborne House, on the Isle of Wight. Wow, what a great place! I could feel the energy there and it's as if Queen Victoria herself was still wandering around. I felt transported back in time. I was walking around when one of the lady tour guides told me that there was a ghost.

"Really," I said, "tell me more."

She said there was a lot of activity on the top floor, "in the children's nursery. It's quite a walk, would you like to take the lift, sir?"

Take the lift in Queen Victoria's Palace? Not at all! I would miss out on all that wonder; all that atmosphere. It was unthinkable taking a modern day lift in such a historic home, although, in hindsight, I wish I had taken the lift as the stairs nearly killed me!

Sure enough, when I eventually got my breath back, yes, she was right. There was definitely spiritual energy up there, but whoever it was, wasn't getting to close to me. Spirit can see mediums very clearly and they were keeping their distance.

Queen Victoria and Prince Albert's private quarters are open to the public, but that wasn't always so. Apparently, Queen Victoria died in her bedroom and after that they put a wrought iron gate up and locked it, allowing no access. In 1951, our late Queen, Elizabeth II, gave permission to open it to the public. I wandered round eventually into her bedroom where she passed back home to the spiritual realms, bless her.

The following Wednesday, I was running one of my development circles. I had run the same one for the previous 10 months (a circle is where like-minded people sit together to grow spiritually). Well the

187

strangest thing happened; we all felt a dramatic change in the temperature; it started to get very cold and I was very aware of someone walking into the room. I am not a name dropper but I swear I felt Queen Victoria standing behind me.

She was a lady with a great sense of humour. To be honest, this shocked me, I thought she always seemed very unhappy and miserable. How wrong could I be? She told me about how they used to run séances in her own rooms in Osborne House! And how she would invite the best known mediums of the time to demonstrate their ability.

She was obviously aware of me visiting her home and made the effort to pay a visit to me at my circle. How wonderful is that? Of course, this could have been my imagination; I mean, it doesn't seem possible, does it? That Queen Victoria would be interested in visiting me; but I can assure you it was real. As I have said, I don't lie; I know what I know.

I am planning another visit.

The Kray Twins

There are no famous spirits; famous spirits don't exist. You're just spirit or spiritual energy and you're the same, but I remember a demonstration many years ago in my local Spiritualist Church.

I was in front of the audience and the church was quite small and busy. There was a tall lady in the front row, reasonably smart and I came to her and it was her uncle who came through.

"Your uncle lived in London," I said.

She agreed.

As I was working with this gentlemanly spirit, I felt like he was a bit of a crook, to say the least.

"He was a bit of a gangster in London he was and he was quite well known," I said.

As she was agreeing with me, I felt two men walk behind me and then stand on either side of me. I suddenly realised that they were the Krays. The renowned 1960s gangsters, the Kray twins, had come in and they were standing either side of me. It was a bit like a British gangster movie.

"Your Uncle knew the Kray twins didn't he?" I asked. "He was a friend of theirs?"

"Yes," she said, "he was. He was very closely connected with the Krays.'

They had come in on the same energy link as her uncle. Her uncle had had a lot of dealings with them in the past.

On that first encounter, I remember saying to them, "You don't scare me."

My guides were around and protecting me, but I heard one of them say, "well, you can run but you can't hide."

"I'm not bothered by you," I said, "you can't hurt me."

I have had other experiences of celebrities as well, not that you could call the Krays celebrity; they were not nice people but that's what they were famous for.

I actually I experienced them again, when I was working at a Spiritualist Church in Brighton. They came through again, slightly worrying for me. I can assure you I am no crook. I wouldn't hurt a fly. The only thing I've ever hit is me thumb with a hammer.

At this particular meeting, there was a lady in the front row and she was in her middle to late sixties. I said to her that she did the same work as I did, that she was a clairvoyant and a medium. I told her that and she agreed. I said I could see her working abroad.

"Yes," she said, "I work a lot in Spain, in the nice part with the wealthy people."

As she said that, I could see the Kray twins walk in on the stage and walk up behind me.

"Your family were connected with the Kray twins, weren't they?" I asked.

"Yes," she replied, "my family were connected with the Krays, you're right."

That was my second experience of the Kray's coming through and they were a particularly unpleasant couple of individuals.

Kenneth Williams

I remember, when I was first getting going, I was doing a demonstration and the lady that was running the church, the secretary, said:

"Oh, my word! I can see Kenneth Williams standing beside you and I think he is working with you."

When I work as a medium, I do bring a lot of humour in and I think it is important. Spirits like it when we laugh.

But I thought that was a bit odd that Kenneth Williams would want to work with me. But I guess I had always liked him as an actor, especially in the Carry on films.

A couple of weeks later I was working at another Spiritualist Church, in the same town.

I was giving messages out and, yet again, at the end of the evening the secretary, who was a completely different woman (they didn't know each other) said:

"You know I caught a glimpse of Kenneth Williams standing around you while you were working this evening."

I thought that is just too much of a coincidence, and as you know, I don't believe in coincidences, so, I think that Kenneth Williams is around. Well, I hope so. I have great child hood memories of the Carry On films. I loved them all.

Sid James

Over the years, I have run development circles. In those circles, I do demonstrations of light trance where I close my eyes, dim the lights slightly but still keep the room lit enough to see my face. The students then watch my face as sometimes, a spirit can 'come in' and morph themselves over my face so that they can be seen by my students. As I remember back, I carried out this demonstration one evening.

I brought myself back and when I was back in a conscious state, one of my students said: "My God while you were in trance your face changed."

"Don't tell me," I said, "but you saw Sid James from the 'Carry On' films."

"I did see Sid James! He was sitting within you and I could see his face so clearly."

Frank Sinatra

Quite a few of the actors that were in the 'Carry On' films have come through, but I've had other celebrities coming through as well.

I can remember doing a demonstration and turning to a gentleman whose father had passed to the world of spirit. His father came through with evidence. I gave his name and how he passed to the world of spirit (how he died) and his life there and I distinctly remember saying:

190

"Your father loved Frank Sinatra."

"Yes he did," he replied.

"Well, Frank Sinatra is here because it's validation that your dad knew him."

So Frank Sinatra came through as well.

The Royal Family

I remember when the Queen Mother died, I was sitting in my lounge watching the TV and I was very aware to my left hand side, across the room, that somebody had wandered in and it was the Queen Mother. I saw her clearly for a brief instance. She stared at me and smiled and then she was gone.

I have had the same experience with Princess Margaret when she passed to the world of spirit. She stopped and looked at me and went on. You see when you die, it doesn't matter if you were famous, wealthy or poor or who you are here, we are all the same in the world of spirit.

There is no hierarchy in terms of what you did here, how rich you were here, how powerful you were or how famous you were. We are all the same in the world of spirit. None of us is any different.

So there you go, it doesn't matter. Even mediums like Doris Stokes or Allan Kardeck working over the centuries that have been famous here are the same as all of us back in spirit. We are all the same when we are back home, there is no fame there. These are just the things we have in this physical realm.

Liberace

I've run many different circles with many different students over the years. But there is always one person that comes in. He usually sits in the corner of the room playing his piano with the biggest grin and laugh on his face and that is Liberace. I have seen him time after time after time.

Bob Marley

A while ago now, I was running a circle. I was linking in, and I saw Bob Marley, the singer walking in and standing behind one of my

191

students (she is very good, clever and a very developed student in many different ways).

"Oh my God," I said, "Bob Marley has just walked in!"

"Oh, I love Bob Marley," she said, "I love his music, his philosophy and his sayings."

That night at about eleven thirty, when I had finished the circle and I was at home, a text came through on my phone. It was the lady I had given the message to earlier that same evening, to say that Bob Marley was around her. She had remembered that she had run a workshop a couple of months before, and she had named her workshop after one of Bob Marley's hits. Bob Marley was around her and giving her inspiration in her life, so much so that she had felt the need to name her workshop after one of his hits. She runs 'Law of Attraction' courses, and he is very much around and working with her, feeding her inspiration.

Barry Sheene

I saw the famous racing biker, Barry Sheene once. During an evening when I was working, there was a lady there in the audience who knew Barry Sheene. I have had many celebrities come through who have now passed. One person I have not yet heard from is Michael Jackson, although many mediums will make claim to this. I will not make claim to any celebrities I have not experienced. I only deal in the truth.

My Legacy

Teaching

I take great pride in, and enjoy teaching people and watching them come on; seeing them as they start to unfold, learn and grow. Often, they'll start to experience things which they've never experienced; they'll start to grow within themselves like they've never grown before. This is because, when you start opening your chakras, your energy centres, you start evolving more spiritually. Lives change and they change in a dramatic way as they start to learn more about spiritual matters and about life as well.

They begin to grow more in their own lives and it's fascinating to watch. I must admit, I take great pride in that, as I've said several times but it is good, it's enjoyable and it is highly rewarding. Also, what happens in these circles, is where you're channelling your guides and spirit and you're learning about energy, then the friendships you make, you'll never forget.

These are friendships that you will have for life and they're bonds you make with people which are never forgotten. You end up with really good friends based over many years, because to share spirituality and to grow spiritually is a wonderful thing. It really expands the human being into lots more areas than they ever felt they could expand into and, as I said, the friendships you make, you keep for life. I have so many friends, now, through the work that I've done spiritually over the years. So many people I can rely on in my life, which is truly fantastic and I love it and am thankful.

Teaching plays a big part in my spiritual life just as demonstrating mediumship, along with my private readings and all my other spiritual work. I also do work occasionally as a healer and I do enjoy healing. I have a guide who comes through and heals with me, I mentioned him before, Dr Feligrew. He is my healing guide who has tremendous energy when he works with me.

I'm Off!

The year is now 2023 and in February, I am off! It is really happening! I am travelling back to the United States of America to follow my dreams. To live there and work full time doing my mediumship.

Where do I go from here, who knows? Who knows what opportunities will open up to me once I am there. I feel that this is what *I have* to do, what *I need* to do. Ultimately, it's what *I want* to do.

I have been in touch with a producer, speaking about a new concept TV show. I have no idea what is around the corner, but I feel excited again, looking forward to what is to come, what more there is for me to learn.

I hope to give many more messages of love, peace, hope and validation of our existence beyond this physical realm.

Mostly, I want to spread love.

My Quotes

Mediumship is the only job you do that doesn't have a script.

We are all one and part of the Great love; that is because we are here together at this time; we are all One.

Go and try everything, well, certainly everything that will benefit you or someone else.

You never know what's possible in your life until you try.

Life is for the living - the dead take care of their own.

Don't forget that love is all you have. Without it, you really have nothing.

In the madness of life, only love truly matters.

Your time here is limited so live a lifetime in a moment.

Holding back the tears is the same as holding back your love.

Bringing light to where there was once darkness.

Death is but a dream and life is just a memory for our soul to keep forever.

It is not the dead that will hurt you, only the living.

Questions And Answers

Q: Is every house haunted?
A: No.

Q: Do spirits watch you when you poop?
A: Ha! That's a funny question. But no.

Q: Can you see animals that have passed to the spirit realms?
A: Yes, I can see animals but I do not try to interact or communicate with them.

Q: Why would a spirit be attached to a house?
A: Some spirits feel possession over their homes and want to keep it for themselves. Sometimes, a spirit is trapped with the house through negative emotions (like being guilt stricken for something they had done while living) and then stuck in the physical plane in spirit form, having not crossed back over to the spiritual realms upon their physical death here.

Q: Are you just a ghosthunter?
A: No. I don't go looking for spirits. It is they who come to me. Or, in some cases, where someone living has asked for help with energies in their home or lives.

Q: Why did you become a professional medium?
A: I didn't plan on becoming a professional medium, I kind of fell into it, so to speak. Once I understood the depths of my gift and that I was mainly just a messenger, well, I knew I had to pass those messages on.

Q: Is the 'God energy' the same as Heaven?
A: Yes. And that is where we are all trying to get to. To that brightest light, that highest level of evolvement.

Q: Can evil spirits trap us or hurt us?
A: No. It is generally us that hurt ourselves.

Q: Do you believe in the Devil?
A: No.

Q: Have you ever worried that you have a serious mental health condition like schizophrenia, rather than communicating with dead people?
A: When I was very young, before I understood what was happening to me, yes, I did worry that there was something wrong with me. But, after I met the psychiatrist, I realised what was happening to me. Once I embraced my gift, that's when I would get validations from others that the evidence I that I was giving through my readings was accurate, I knew for sure that I was not mentally ill.

Q: What is the question that you are asked most by those who seek your help spiritually?
A: Most asked question is probably 'is there anyone around me?'

Q: Is there a secret to opening your mind to communicate with someone in the spiritual realms?
A: For the average person, not really, but it depends on the individual's level of sensitivity.
Mediums are born with their gift.

Q: If you can sometimes see into the future, can you see your own future?
A: I guess I could, but then the mind only sees what it wants us to see. Also, my emotional and mental state at the time would also affect what I could/would envision. So therefore, no, not accurately anyway.

Q: Are you ever able to relax or do you always have spirits reaching out to you?
A: Now that I have developed my gift a lot more, I can relax and shut out spirit. Now, I have to 'link in' and 'open up' to communicate with the spiritual realms, which is better for me.

Q: Have you ever seen that something bad is going to happen to someone?
A: Yes, I have, unfortunately. I've even seen visions of people passing back to spirit. But, as I mentioned earlier, if a medium sees something bad, they should not tell the receiver as it could, effectively, ruin their lives. A medium has an ethical and moral

obligation to only pass on messages of love, peace, happiness and validation that there is some form of life after death in this physical realm.

Q: When you see spirits, do they look see-through or just like us?
A: To be honest, it varies. Some look just like a solid, normal person, others look somewhat translucent.

Q: What makes you different from all the fake mediums out there?
A: I have had many validations of the information that I have received from spirit and passed on to loved ones still with us here. That is enough proof, I believe.

Q: Did you ever worry about 'coming out' as a medium for fear of judgement from others?
A: No, never.

Q: Have you ever been visited by a spirit that you know personally?
A: Yes, I have. My good friend, Peter Richards, who I have mentioned a lot within this book, has visited me several times since he passed back to spirit.

Q: Can a spirit who has only just passed make contact with you or do they have to have been passed for a certain amount of time?
A: Yes. I once done a reading and a man came through who was having his wake that same day!

Contact

www.nigelgaff.com

Facebook: The English Medium

Instagram: @the_english_medium

Printed in Great Britain
by Amazon